General Stuart in 1854, from an ambrotype owned by Mrs. J.E. B. Stuart, which is here reproduced for the first time.

Life of General J. E. B. Stuart

For Young Readers

By Mrs. Mary L. Williamson

Author of Life of Lee, Life of Jackson, and Life of Washington

Edited And Arranged For School Use
By
E. O. Wiggins
English Department, Lynchburg High School, Virginia

REPRINTED BY

Wake Forest, NC
www.scuppernongpress.com

Life of General J. E. B. Stuart For Young Readers
By Mrs. Mary L. Williamson

Edited by Frank B. Powell, III

©2025 The Scuppernong Press

First Printing

The Scuppernong Press
PO Box 1724
Wake Forest, NC 27588
www.scuppernongpress.com

Cover and book design by Frank B. Powell, III

All rights reserved

Printed in the United States of America

No part of this book may be reproduced or transmitted in any form or by any means, electronic or mechanical, including photocopying, recording, or by any information and storage and retrieval system, without written permission from the editor and/or publisher.

International Standard Book Number ISBN 978-1-942806-80-6

Library of Congress Control Number: 2026930401

CONTENTS

Chapter	Page
Foreword	iii
Preface	v
Acknowledgements	vii
Introduction	1
Chapter I Youthful Days	3
Chapter II A Lieutenant in the United States Cavalry	9
Chapter III A Colonel of Confederate Cavalry	17
Chapter IV A Brigadier General: The Peninsular Campaign and the Chickahominy Raid	23
Chapter V A Major General: Camp Life and the Second Battle of Manassas	37
Chapter VI The Maryland Campaign	43
Chapter VII The Chambersburg Raid	51
Chapter VIII The Cavalry at Culpeper and Fredericksburg	59
Chapter IX Chancellorsville	67
Chapter X The Battle of Brandy Station	75
Chapter XI The Gettysburg Campaign	83
Chapter XII Final Campaigns and Death	91
Chapter XIII Some Tributes to Stuart	105
Suggestive Questions	113
The Organization of an Army	119
Word List	121

General J. E. B. Stuart

FOREWORD

The "Eyes and Ears of Lee" became the name of General J. E. B. Stuart's efforts. He played an important role in the battles of the Army of Northern Virginia. He did a great job as you will read in these pages. If fact, he also became known as the "Last Cavalier" because of his daring and dashing movements around Federal forces.

Readers will also learn about some of the causes of the War Between the States and what drove Southerns to take up arms to defend home and hearth from invasion.

This book has long been out of print, but after recently discovering it, we felt the need to republish it for a new generation of young readers. This edition is reprinted in a modern typeface with small changes to modern punctuation and grammar standards. Most of the original illustrations are included as printed in the 1914 edition.

This is a companion to Mrs. Williamson's *The Life of General Robert E. Lee In Easy Words For Children* and *The Life of General T. J. "Stonewall" Jackson In Easy Words For The Young*. She intended for these small books to serve as supplemental textbooks to be used in public schools. Of course, this will not happen in today's Marxist, cancel culture, public/government schools. But, parents can, and should, use this book to teach their children about one of the greatest men in American history.

We hope you enjoy our efforts. Please share this book with your children, grandchildren, nieces and nephews, grand nieces and nephews, cousins and other young people you may know. For if we don't share our history, it will die with us.

— *Frank B. Powell, III*
Editor

PREFACE

Some years ago, to fill what appeared to me a need in our literature for children, I made a study of the lives and campaigns of General R. E. Lee and of General Stonewall Jackson and prepared, for very young readers, histories of those great commanders. In performing these tasks, I became interested in the combats and maneuvers of General Lee's chief of cavalry, Major General J. E. B. Stuart, who has been justly called "the eyes and ears of Lee." As the years go by, I find no book in print recounting to children his wonderful feats and valorous service, or explaining to them the part played in the battles of Lee and Jackson by the Stuart Cavalry Corps and Horse Artillery whose exploits hold a brilliant place in modern military tactics. To make good this omission, I have prepared this little life of Stuart, in the hope it will not only pass on the story of military deeds as captivating as any in history, but warm the hearts of rising generations to lives of courage and devotion. In the later stages of my work, Miss Evelina O. Wiggins has been associated, contributing various materials, obtaining three pictures and several interesting letters of General Stuart's, and making available Mrs. J. E. B. Stuart's criticism of the manuscript. Miss Wiggins has also rendered the aid of adapting the book to the practical needs of the schoolroom. Her experience and position as a teacher make the latter service highly valuable.

— Mary Lynn Williamson
New Market, VA
September 1, 1914

ACKNOWLEDGMENTS

The publishers wish to acknowledge their obligations to Mrs. H. B. McClellan for permission to use material from her husband's book, *Life and Campaigns of General J. E. B. Stuart*; to General T. T. Munford and to Judge Theodore S. Garnett for information and pictures; to Mr. J. E. B. Stuart and the Confederate Museum, Richmond, VA, for permission to make photographic copies of the personal relics of General Stuart in the Museum; and to Mrs. J. E. B. Stuart for the ambrotype and letters of General Stuart which she allowed to be copied for use in this book and for the invaluable aid of her careful critical reading of the manuscript.

INTRODUCTION

Henry of Navarre was a famous French king who led his forces to a glorious victory in a civil war. An English writer, Lord Macaulay, wrote a stirring poem in which a French soldier is represented as describing this battle. Here is his picture of the great, beloved king: —

"The King is come to marshal us, in all his armor drest, And he has bound a snow-white plume upon his gallant crest. He looked upon his people and a tear was in his eye, He looked upon the traitors and his glance was stern and high; Right graciously he smiled on us, as rolled from wing to wing, Down all our line a deafening shout, 'God save our lord, the King!'

"And if my standard bearer fall, — as fall full well he may, For never saw I promise yet of such a bloody fray — Press where you see my white plume shine amidst the ranks of war. And be your oriflamme today the helmet of Navarre.'

> *'A thousand spurs are striking deep, a thousand spears in rest,*
> *A thousand knights are pressing close behind the snow- white crest;*
> *And in they burst and on they rushed, while like a guiding star.*
> *Amidst the thickest carnage blazed the helmet of Navarre."*

These lines about the French king of the sixteenth century are often quoted in describing a gallant cavalry leader of our own country. As we read them, we see the Confederate general, "Jeb" Stuart, his cavalry hat looped back on one side with a long black ostrich plume which his troopers always saw in the forefront of the charge. His men would follow that plume anywhere, at any time, and when you read this story of his life, you will not wonder that he inspired their absolute devotion.

You have read about the lives of the peerless commander General Robert E. Lee, and his great lieutenant General Stonewall Jackson. In these you have learned something about the movements of the great body of our army, the infantry; but the infantry, even with such able commanders as Lee and Jackson, needed the aid of the cavalry and the artillery. It is with these two latter divisions of the army we deal in studying the life of General Stuart. As chief of cavalry and commander of the famous Stuart Horse Artillery, he served as eyes and ears to the commanding generals. He kept them informed about the location and movements of the Federals, screened the location of the Confederate troops, felt the way, protected the flank and rear when the army was on the march, and made quick raids into the Federal territory or around their army to secure supples and information as well as to mislead them concerning the proposed movements of Confederate forces. A heavy responsibility rested on the cavalry, and General Stuart and his men were engaged in many small but severe battles and skirmishes in which the army as a whole did not take part.

> *"To horse, to horse! the sabers gleam.*
> *High sounds our bugle call,*
> *Combined by honor's sacred tie,*
> *Our watchword, 'laws and liberty!'*
> *Forward to do or die."*
> — Sir Walter Scott

LIFE OF J. E. B. STUART

CHAPTER I
YOUTHFUL DAYS
1833-'54

James Ewell Brown Stuart, commonly known as "Jeb" Stuart from the first three initials of his name, was born in Patrick County, Virginia, February 6, 1833. On each side of his family, he could point to a line of ancestors who had served their country well in war and peace and from whom he inherited his high ideals of duty, patriotism, and religion.

He was of Scotch descent and his ancestors belonged to a clan of note in the history of Scotland. From Scotland a member of this clan went to Ireland.

About the year 1726, Jeb Stuart's great-great-grandfather, Archibald Stuart, fled from Londonderry, Ireland, to the wilds of Pennsylvania, in order to escape religious persecution.

Eleven years later, he removed from Pennsylvania to Augusta County, Virginia, where he became a large landholder. At Tinkling Spring Church, the graves of the immigrant and his wife may still be seen.

Archibald Stuart's second son, Alexander, joined the Continental Army and fought with signal bravery during the whole of the War of the Revolution. After the war, he practiced law. He showed his interest in education by becoming one of the founders of Liberty Hall, at Lexington, Virginia, a school which afterwards became Washington College and has now grown into Washington and Lee University.

Ruins of Liberty Hall Academy, at Lexington, VA.

His youngest son who bore his name, was also a lawyer; he held positions of trust in his native state, Virginia, as well as in Illinois and Missouri where he held the responsible and honored position of a United States judge.

Our general's father, Archibald Stuart, the son of Judge Stuart, after a brief military career in the War of 1812, became a successful lawyer. His wit and eloquence soon won him distinction, and his district sent him as representative to the Congress of the United States where he served four years.

There is an interesting story told about General Stuart's mother's grandfather, William Letcher. He had enraged the Loyalists, or Tories, on the North Carolina border, by a defeat that he and a little company of volunteers had inflicted on them in the War of the Revolution. One day in June, 1780, as Mrs. Letcher was alone at home with her baby girl, only six weeks old, a stranger, dressed as a hunter and carrying a gun in his hand, appeared at the door and asked for Letcher. While his wife was explaining that he would be at home in a short time, he entered and asked the man to be seated.
The latter, however, raised his gun, saying: "I demand you in the name of the king."
When Letcher tried to seize the gun, the Tory fired and the patriot fell mortally wounded, in the presence of his young wife and babe.

Bethenia Letcher, the tiny fatherless babe, grew to womanhood and married David Pannill; and her daughter, Elazabeth Letcher Pannill, married Archibald Stuart, the father of our hero.
Mrs. Archibald Stuart inherited from her grandfather, William Letcher, a large estate in Patrick County. The place, commanding fine views of the Blue Ridge mountains, was called Laurel Hill, and here in a comfortable old mansion set amid a grove of oak trees, Jeb Stuart was born and spent the earlier years of his boyhood.
Mrs. Stuart was a great lover of flowers and surrounding the house was a beautiful old-fashioned flower garden, where Jeb, who loved flowers as much as his mother did, spent many happy days. He always loved this boyhood home and often thought of it during the hard and stirring years of war. Once near the close of the war, he told his brother he would like nothing better, when the long struggle was at an end, than to go back to the old home and live a quiet, peaceful life.

When Jeb was fourteen years old, he was sent to school in Wytheville, and in 1848 he entered Emory and Henry College. Here, under the influence of a religious revival, he joined the Methodist church, but about ten years later he became a member of the Episcopal church of which his wife was a member.

Though always gay and high-spirited, Stuart even as a boy possessed a deep religious sentiment which grew in strength as he grew in years and kept his heart pure and his hands clean through the many temptations that beset him in the freedom and conviviality of army life. A promise he made his mother never to taste strong drink was kept faithfully to his death, and none of his soldiers ever heard him use an oath even in the heat of battle. His gallantry, boldness, and continual gayety and good nature, coupled with his high Christian virtues, caused all who came in contact with him not only to love but to respect and admire him.

Emory And Henry College About 1850

He left Emory and Henry College in 1850 and entered the United States Military Academy at West Point where he had received an appointment.

At this time, Colonel Robert E. Lee was superintendent at West Point. Young Stuart spent many pleasant hours at the home of the superintendent where he was a great favorite with the ladies of the family. Custis Lee, the eldest son of Colonel Lee, was Stuart's best friend while he was a student at the Academy.

An interesting incident is told about Stuart while he was on a vacation from West Point. Mr. Benjamin B. Minor of Richmond, had a case to be tried at Williamsburg, and when he arrived at the hotel it was so crowded that he was put in an "omnibus" room, so called because it contained three double beds.

Late in the afternoon when the stage drove up, he saw three young cadets step from it and he soon found that they were to share with him the "omnibus" room.

He went to bed early, but put a lamp on the table by the head of his bed and got out his papers to go over his case. After awhile the three cadets came in laughing and singing, and soon they were all three piled into one bed where they continued to laugh and joke in uproarious spirits.

Finally one of them said, "See here, fellows, we have had our fun long enough and we are disturbing that gentleman over there; let us hush up and go to sleep."

"No need for that, boys," said Mr. Minor, "I have just finished."

Then as he tells us he 'pitched in' and had a good time with them.

The cadet who had shown such thoughtfulness and courtesy was young Jeb Stuart who as Mr. Minor discovered was one of his wife's cousins. He was very much pleased with the boy and invited him to come to Richmond. Stuart accepted the invitation and called several times at the Minor home.

He explained to Mr. Minor his plan for an invention which was to be called "Stuart's lightning horse-hitcher" and to be used in Indian raids. He excited Mr. Minor's admiration because he had such gallant and genial courtesy and professional pride. He wanted even then to accomplish something useful and important to his country and himself.

General Fitzhugh Lee, who was at West Point with Stuart, and who later served under General Stuart as a trusted commander, tells us as a cadet he was remarkable for "strict attendance to military duties, and erect, soldierly bearing, an immediate and almost thankful acceptance of a challenge to fight any cadet who might in any way feel himself aggrieved, and a clear, metallic, ringing voice."

Although the boys called him a "Bible class man" and "Beauty Stuart," it was in good-natured boyish teasing; where he felt it to be intended differently or where his high standards of conduct seemed to be sneered at, he was well able with his quick temper and superb physical strength to teach the offender a lesson.

As 'Fitz' Lee tells us, Stuart was always ready to accept a challenge, but he did not fight without good cause, and his father, a fair-minded and intelligent man, approved of his son's course in these fisticuff encounters. Between his father and himself there was the best kind of comradeship and sympathy, and young Stuart was always ready to consult his father before taking any important step in life. The decision as to what he should do when he left West Point, however, was left to him, and just after his graduation he wrote home that he had decided to enter the regular army instead of becoming a lawyer.

"Each profession has its labors and rewards," he wrote, "and in making the selection I shall rely upon Him whose judgment cannot err, for it is not with the man that walketh to direct his steps."

Meanwhile, by his daring and skill in horsemanship, his diligence in his studies, and his ability to command, he had risen rapidly from the position of corporal to that of captain, and then to the rank of cavalry sergeant which is the highest rank in that arm of the service at West Point. He graduated thirteenth in a class of forty-six, and started his brief but brilliant military career well equipped with youth, courage, skill, and a firm reliance on the love and wisdom of God.

From daguerreotype in Confederate Museum, Richmond, VA.
J. E. B. Stuart when a student at West Point.

BADGE OF WEST POINT GRADUATES

The arms of the United States Academy, suspended by a ribbon of black, gray, and gold from a bar bearing the date of the graduate's class.

CHAPTER II
A LIEUTENANT IN THE UNITED STATES CAVALRY
1854-'61

Most of Stuart's time from his graduation at West Point until the outbreak of the War of Secession was spent in military service along the southern and western borders of our country. During this period, there was almost constant warfare between Indians and frontier settlers. Stuart had many interesting adventures in helping to protect the settlers and to drive the Indians back into their own territory. The training he received at this time helped to develop him into a great cavalry and artillery leader.

The autumn after he left West Point, Stuart was commissioned second lieutenant in a regiment of mounted riflemen on duty in western Texas. He reached Fort Clark in December, just in time to join an expedition against the Apache Indians who had been giving the settlers a great deal of trouble. The small force to which he was attached pushed boldly into the Indian country north of the Rio Grande. It was not long before the young officer's skill and determination received a severe test. The trail the expedition followed led to the top of a steep and rugged ridge which to the troopers' astonishment dropped abruptly two thousand feet to an extensive valley. The precipice formed of huge columns of vertical rock, at first seemed impassable, but they soon found a narrow and dangerous Indian trail— the kind which is called a "mule-path" — winding to the base of the mighty cliff. The officers and advance guard dismounted and led their horses down the steep path which scarcely afforded footing for a man and passed on to choose a bivouac for the night. A little later, Lieutenant Stuart, with a rear guard of fifty rangers detailed to assist him, reached the top of the ridge, with their single piece of artillery. Stuart worked his way down the trail alone, hoping that when he reached the foot he would find that the major in charge of the expedition had left word the gun was to be abandoned as it seemed impossible to carry it down the precipice. No such order awaited him, however, and the young officer determined to get the gun down in spite of all difficulties. He noted well the dangers of the way as he regained the top and, having had the mules unhitched and led down by some of the men, he unlimbered

Life of General J. E. B. Stuart

the gun and started the captain of the rangers and twenty-five men down with the limber. He himself took charge of the gun and, with the help of the remaining men, lifted it over huge rocks and lowered it by lariat ropes over impassable places until it was finally brought safely to the valley below.

The major had taken it for granted Stuart would leave the gun at the top of the precipice and was amazed when just at supper time it was brought safely into camp. Such ingenuity, grit, and determination were qualities which promised that the young officer would develop into a skillful and reliable leader.

Carrying the gun down the 'mule-path'

A few days later, the command encamped for the night in a narrow valley between high ridges. The camp fires were burning brightly and the cooks were preparing supper when a sudden violent gust of wind swept through the valley and scattering the fire set the whole prairie into a moving flame. With such rapidity did the fire sweep over the camp that the men were unable to save anything except their horses, and in a deplorable condition the expedition was forced to return to the camp in Texas.

In May, 1855, Stuart was transferred to the First Regiment of cavalry, with the rank of second lieutenant. In July, this regiment was ordered to Fort Leavenworth, Kansas; and in September, it went on a raid, under the leadership of Colonel E. V. Sumner, against some Indians who had disturbed the white settlers. The savages retreated to their mountain strongholds and the regiment returned to the fort without fighting.

While on this expedition, Stuart learned with deep distress of the death of his wise and affectionate father. It had been only a few weeks before that Mr. Stuart had written to approve his son's marriage to Miss

Flora Cooke, daughter of Colonel Philip St. George Cooke who was commandant at Fort Riley. The marriage was celebrated at that place, November 14, 1855.

At this time, there was serious trouble in Kansas between the two political parties which were fighting to decide whether Kansas should become a free or a slave state. Stuart, who had been promoted to the rank of first lieutenant, was stationed at Fort Leavenworth in 1856-'57. Here he was involved in many skirmishes and local raids. It was at this time he encountered the outlaw "Ossawatomie" Brown of whom we shall hear again a little later.

Stuart passed uninjured through the Kansas contest, and in 1857 entered upon another Indian war against the Cheyenne warriors who were attacking the western settlers. In the chief battle of this campaign, the Indians were routed, but Lieutenant Stuart was wounded while rescuing a brother officer who was attacked by an Indian.

Here is Stuart's own account of the fight as given in a letter to his wife, which she has kindly allowed us to copy:

"Very few of the company horses were fleet enough after the march, besides my own Brave Dan, to keep in reach of the Indians mounted on fresh ponies As long as Dan held out I was foremost, but after a chase of five miles he failed and I had to mount a private's horse and continue the pursuit.

"When I overtook the rear of the enemy again, I found Lomax in imminent danger from an Indian who was on foot and in the act of shooting him. I rushed to the rescue, and succeeded in firing at him in time, wounding him in his thigh. He fired at me in return with an Allen's revolver, but missed. My shots were now exhausted, and I called on some men approaching to rush up with their pistols and kill him. They rushed up, but fired without hitting.

"About this time I observed Stanley and McIntyre close by; the former said, 'Wait, I'll fetch him,' and dismounted from his horse so as to aim deliberately, but in dismounting, his pistol accidentally discharged the last load he had. He began, however, to snap the empty barrels at the Indian who was walking deliberately up to him with his revolver pointed.

"I could not stand that, but drawing my saber rushed on the monster, inflicting a severe wound across his head, that I think would have severed any other man's, but simultaneous with that he fired his last barrel within a foot of me, the ball taking effect in the breast, but by the mercy of God glancing to the left and lodging so far inside that it cannot be felt. I rejoice to inform you that it is not regarded as at all fatal or dangerous, though I may be confined to my bed for weeks."

After this battle, all of the force pursued the Indians, except a small detachment under Captain Foote, which was left behind to guard the wounded for whom the surgeon established rough hospital quarters on the banks of a beautiful, winding creek. Here Stuart spent nearly a week confined to his cot, and as he wrote his wife at the time, the only books that he had to read during the long, weary days were his *Prayer Book* — which was not neglected — and his *Army Regulations*. A few pages of *Harper's Weekly* that some one happened to have were considered quite a treasure.

At the end of about ten days, some Pawnee guides who had been attached to the expedition brought orders for this little detachment to leave the camp where it was exposed to attacks from the wandering bands of Cheyenne Indians and go back to Fort Kearny a hundred miles away.

Stuart was just able to sit on his horse again, yet we shall see that in spite of his wound he was the life and salvation of the little party.

The Pawnees said they were only four days distant from the fort, but the second day these unreliable guides deserted and the soldiers were lost in a heavy fog, without a compass. They were forced to depend on a Cheyenne prisoner for information. After four days' fruitless and difficult marching through the forest, Stuart, who believed the guard was willfully misleading them, volunteered to go ahead with a small force, find the fort, and send back help for those who were still suffering too seriously from their wounds to keep up on a rapid and uncertain march.

After many dangers and deep anxiety on his part, taking his course by the stars when the fog lifted at night and working his way through it as best he could by day, he finally reached Fort Kearny. The Pawnees had come in three days before, and scouting parties had been searching for Captain Foote's command about which much anxiety was felt. Help was immediately sent them, and as a result of Stuart's indomitable will and able services, the little party was rescued and brought safely to the fort.

From the autumn of 1857 until the summer of 1860, Stuart was stationed at Fort Riley. During these three years, there were few skirmishes with the Indians and Stuart had leisure to perfect the invention of a saber

From McClure's Magazine, Indians of the Plains.

attachment that he had been thinking of ever since his student days at West Point. This invention was bought and patented by the government in October, 1859, while the inventor was on leave of absence in Virginia, visiting his mother and his friends.

It was on the night of the sixteenth of this same October that a band of twenty men, under the leadership of John Brown, seized the United States arsenal at Harper's Ferry. Brown was a fanatic who believed all slaves should be set free and who had taken an active part in the recent disturbances in Kansas. After seizing the arsenal at Harper's Ferry, he sent out his followers during the night to arrest certain citizens and to call to arms the slaves on the surrounding plantations. About sixty citizens were arrested and imprisoned in the engine house, within the confines of the armory, but the slaves, either through fear or through distrust of Brown and his schemes, refused to obey his summons.

The next morning as soon as news of the seizure of Harper's Ferry spread over the country, armed men came against Brown from all directions. Before night he and his followers took refuge in the engine house, but it was so crowded he was obliged to release all but ten of his prisoners.

When the news of Brown's raid was telegraphed to Washington, Lieutenant Stuart, who was at the capital attending to the sale of his patent saber attachment, was requested to bear a secret order to Lieutenant Colonel Robert E. Lee, his old superintendent at West Point, who was then at his home, Arlington, near Washington City. Stuart learned Colonel Lee had been ordered to command the marines who were being sent to suppress the insurrection at Harper's Ferry, and he at once offered to act as aid-de-camp. Colonel, Lee, who remembered Stuart well as a cadet, immediately accepted his offer of service.

Arsenal at Harper's Ferry

Upon arriving at Harper's Ferry on the night of October 17, they found John Brown and his men were still in the engine house, defying the citizen soldiers who surrounded the building. Colonel Lee proceeded to surround the engine house with the marines; at daylight, wishing to avoid bloodshed, he sent Lieutenant Stuart to demand the surrender of the fanatical men, promising to protect them from the fury of the citizens until he could give them up to the United States government.

When Lieutenant Stuart advanced to the parley. Brown, who had assumed the name of Smith, opened the door four or five inches only, placed his body against it, and held a loaded carbine in such a position that, as he stated afterward, he might have "wiped Stuart out like a mosquito." Immediately the young officer recognized in the so-called Smith the identical John, or "Ossawatomie," Brown who had caused so much trouble in Kansas. Brown refused Colonel Lee's terms and demanded permission to march out with his men and prisoners and proceed as far as the second toll-gate. Here, he declared, he would free his prisoners and if Colonel Lee wished to pursue he would fight to the bitter end.

Stuart said these terms could not be accepted and urged him to surrender at once. When Brown refused, Stuart waved his cap, the signal agreed upon, and the marines advanced, battered down the doors, and engaged in a hand-to-hand fight with the insurgents. Ten of Brown's men were killed by the marines and all the rest, including Brown himself, were wounded.

That same day. Lieutenant Stuart, under Colonel Lee's orders, went to a farm about four miles and a half away that Brown had rented and brought back a number of pikes with which Brown had intended to arm the negroes. Colonel Lee was then ordered back to Washington and Stuart went with him. John Brown and seven of his men were tried, were found guilty of treason, and were hanged.

The John Brown Raid cast a great gloom over the country. While many people in the North regarded Brown as a martyr to the cause of emancipation, the Southern people were justly indignant at the thought that their lives and property were no longer safe from the plots of the Abolition party which Brown had represented. The bitter feelings aroused by this affair culminated, in 1861, in the bloody War of Secession.

CHAPTER III
A COLONEL OF CONFEDERATE CAVALRY
1861

There seems to have been no doubt in the mind of Lieutenant Stuart as to what he should do in the event of Virginia's withdrawal from the Union. As soon as he heard the Old Dominion had seceded, he forwarded to the War Department his resignation as an officer in the United States army, and hastening to Richmond, he enlisted in the militia of his native state. Like most other Southerners, he preferred poverty and hardships in defense of the South to all the honors and wealth which the United States government could bestow.

On May 10, 1861, Stuart was commissioned as lieutenant colonel of infantry and was ordered to report to Colonel T. J. Jackson at Harper's Ferry. While he was at Harper's Ferry, Stuart organized several troops of cavalry to assist the infantry and he was soon transferred to this branch of the service.

On May 15, General Joseph E. Johnston was sent by the Confederate government to take command of all the forces at Harper's Ferry; while Colonel Jackson, who had previously been in command of the place, was assigned charge of the Virginia regiments afterwards famous as the "Stonewall Brigade." General Johnston found he was unable to hold the town against the advancing Federal force; so he destroyed the railway bridge and retired with his guns and stores to Bunker Hill, twelve miles from Winchester, where he offered battle to the Federals. They declined to fight and withdrew to the north bank of the Potomac River.

When the Federals under General Patterson again crossed the river, General Jackson with his brigade was sent forward to support the cavalry under Stuart and to destroy the railway engines and cars at Martinsburg. Jackson then remained with his brigade near Martinsburg, while his front was protected by Colonel Stuart with a regiment of cavalry.

On July 1, General Patterson advanced toward General Jackson, who went forward to meet him, with only the Fifth Regiment, several companies of cavalry, and one piece of artillery. The Confederate general posted his men behind a farm house and barn, and held back Patterson so well that he threw forward an entire division to overpower the small force of

Jackson. The latter then fell back slowly to the main body of his troops, with the trifling loss of two men wounded and nine missing.

While supporting Jackson in this first battle in the Shenandoah valley, known as the battle of Haines' Farm or Falling Waters, Colonel Stuart had a remarkable adventure. Riding alone in advance of his men, he came suddenly out of a piece of woods at a point where he could see a force of Federal infantry on the other side of the fence. Without a moment's hesitation, he rode boldly forward and ordered the Federal soldiers to pull down the bars.

They obeyed and he immediately rode through to the other side, and in peremptory tones said, "Throw down your arms or you are dead men."

The raw troops were so overcome by Stuart's boldness and commanding tones that they obeyed at once and then marched as he directed through the gap in the fence. Before they recovered from their astonishment, Stuart had them surrounded by his own force which had come up in the meantime, thus capturing more than forty men — almost an entire company.

After some marching backward and forward. General Johnston retired to Winchester; while General Patterson moved farther south to Smithfield as if he intended to attack in that direction. Stuart with his small force was now compelled to watch a front of more than fifty miles, in order to report promptly the movements of the Federals, yet he did this so efficiently that later on when General Johnston was ordered west, he wrote to Stuart:

"How can I eat, sleep, or rest in peace, without you upon the outpost?"

General Johnston now received a call for help from General Beauregard who commanded a Confederate army of twenty thousand men at Manassas Junction. Beauregard was confronted by a Federal army of thirty-five thousand men, including nearly all of the United States regulars east of the Rocky Mountains. This army, commanded by General McDowell, was equipped with improved firearms and had fine uniforms, good tents, and everything money could buy to make good soldiers. The North was very proud of this fine army and fully expected it to crush Beauregard and to sweep on to Richmond.

Beauregard was indeed in danger. He had a smaller army and his infantry was armed, for the most part, with old-fashioned smooth-bore muskets, and his cavalry with sabers and shotguns. One company of cavalry was armed only with the pikes of John Brown, which had been stored at Harper's Ferry. Beauregard stationed his forces in line of battle along the banks of Bull Run from the Stone Bridge to Union Mills, a distance of eight miles. On July 18, the Federals tried to force Blackburn's Ford on Bull Run, but were repulsed with heavy loss. Beauregard, knowing the attack would be renewed the next day, sent a message to Johnston at Winchester, sixty miles away.

"If you are going to help me, now is the time," was Beauregard's message.

Two days before, Stuart had been transferred to the cavalry, with a commission as colonel, and he entered at once upon his arduous labors. At first he had in his command only twenty-one officers and three hundred and thirteen men, raw to military discipline and poorly armed with the guns they had used in hunting, but all were fine horsemen and good shots.

General Johnston, leaving Stuart with a little band of troopers to conceal his movements, immediately commenced his march from Winchester to Manassas. So skillfully did Colonel Stuart do his work that General Patterson was not aware of General Johnston's departure until Sunday, July 21, when the great battle of Manassas was fought. Owing to a collision which had blocked the railway, some of the infantry did not reach Manassas until near the close of the battle, but the cavalry and the artillery marched all the way and arrived in time to render effective service during the entire battle.

It was at Manassas that General Jackson won his name of "Stonewall" because of the wonderful stand his brigade made, just when it seemed the Federals were about to overcome the Confederates. But we are concerned particularly with the movements of the cavalry which rendered fine service, protecting each flank of the army. Colonel Stuart, with only two companies of cavalry, protected the left flank from assault after assault. At one time Stuart boldly charged the Federal right and drove back a company of Zouaves resplendent in their blue and scarlet uniforms and white turbans.

General Early, who arrived on the field about three o'clock in the afternoon and assisted in holding the left flank, said, "But for Stuart's presence there, I am of the opinion that my brigade would have arrived too late to be of any use. Stuart did as much toward saving the First Manassas as any subordinate who participated in it."

General Jackson, in his report of the battle, said: "Apprehensive lest my flanks be turned, I sent orders to Colonels Stuart and Radford of the cavalry to secure them. Colonel Stuart and that part of his command with him deserve great praise for the promptness with which they moved to my left and secured my flank from the enemy, and by driving them back."

Thus we see at the very crisis of the battle, Stuart with only a small force aided largely in gaining the great victory. When he saw the Federals fleeing from all parts of the field, he pursued them for twelve miles, taking many prisoners and securing much booty.

After the battle of First Manassas, the main armies were inactive for many months; but the Confederate cavalry was kept busy in frequent skirmishes with the Federal pickets and in raids toward the Potomac river. Stuart took possession of Munson's Hill, near Washington, and for several weeks sent out his pickets within sight of the dome of the Capitol.

In a letter from General F. E. Paxton, of the Stonewall Brigade, we find this interesting mention of Colonel Stuart and his life at the outpost: "Yesterday I was down the road about ten miles, and, from a hill in the possession of our troops, had a good view of the dome of the Capitol, some five or six miles distant. The city was not visible, because of the woods coming between. I saw the sentinel of the enemy in the field below me, and about half a mile off and not far on this side, our own sentinels. They fire sometimes at each other. Mrs. Stuart, wife of the colonel who has charge of our outpost, visits him occasionally— having a room with friends a few miles inside the outpost. Whilst there looking at the Capitol, I saw two of his little children playing as carelessly as if they were at home. A dangerous place, you will think, for women and children."

Mrs. Stuart, however, was a soldier's daughter and a soldier's wife, and she took advantage of every opportunity to be with her husband at his headquarters. During the beginning of the war, before the engagements with the Federals became frequent, she was often able to be with her husband or to board at some home near which he was stationed. Although he was a favorite with women, there was no woman who, in General Stuart's eyes, could compare with his wife, and he was never happier than when with her and his children. When the general's duties compelled him to be away from her, two days seldom passed that Mrs. Stuart did not hear from him by letter or telegram.

On September 11, Stuart's forces encountered a raiding party which was forced to retire with a loss of two killed and thirteen wounded, while Stuart lost neither man nor horse.

During the summer, Stuart had been ordered to report to General James Longstreet who commanded the advance of the Confederate army.

General Longstreet in a letter to President Davis said of Stuart: "He is a rare man, wonderfully endowed by nature with the qualities necessary for an officer of light cavalry. Calm, firm, acute, active, and enterprising, I know no one more competent than he to estimate events at their true value. If you add a brigade of cavalry to this army, you will find no better brigadier general to command it."

Picketed cavalry horse

Stuart's gauntlets
From originals in Confederate Museum Richmond, VA.

Stuart's cavalry boots
From originals in Confederate Museum Richmond, VA.

CHAPTER IV

A BRIGADIER GENERAL: THE PENINSULAR CAMPAIGN AND THE CHICKAHOMINY RAID 1861-'62

On September 24, 1861, Stuart received his promotion as brigadier general. His brigade included four Virginia regiments, one North Carolina regiment, and the Jeff Davis Legion of Cavalry. These regiments were composed of high-spirited, brave young men who could ride dashingly and shoot with the skill of back-woodsmen, but who were for the most part untrained in military affairs. Stuart, however, was an untiring drill- master and by his personal efforts he developed his brigade into a command of capable and devoted soldiers.

The young general was not yet twenty-nine years old. He was of medium height, had winning blue eyes, long silken bronze beard and mustache, and a musical voice. He usually wore gauntlets, high cavalry boots, a broad-brimmed felt hat caught up on one side by a black ostrich plume, and a tight-fitting cavalry coat that he called his "Fighting jacket." He rode as if he had been born in the saddle.

Fitz Lee, who served under him, said: "His strong figure, his big brown beard, his piercing, laughing blue eyes, black leather, the 'fighting jacket' as he termed it, the tall cavalry boots, formed one of the most jubilant and striking pictures in the war."

Later on, John Esten Cooke described Stuart thus: "His 'fighting jacket' shone with dazzling buttons, and was covered with gold braid; his hat was looped up with a golden star and decorated with a black ostrich plume; his fine buff gauntlets reached to the elbow; around his waist was tied a splendid yellow sash and his spurs were of pure gold."

One who formed an opinion of him from a casual glance might have thought he was merely a gay young fop, fond of handsome and even showy dress. But his friends and his enemies knew better. Gay and even boyish as he was when off duty, loving music and good cheer, his men knew the instant the bugles called him he would become the calm, daring, farsighted commander, leading them to glorious deeds. No leader of the Southern army was more feared by the Federal troops or more admired by the commanders of the Federal cavalry — Sheridan, Pleasanton, Buford, and others — than Stuart whom they nicknamed "the Yellow Jacket." He seemed to fly from place to place, guarding the Confederate line and charging the Federals at the most unexpected times and places; gayly dressed as that brilliant-colored insect, he was as sharp and sudden in attack.

Possessing the daring courage which is necessary for a great cavalry leader, he was so wary and farsighted that he won the respect of conservative leaders as well as the confidence of his men. And in victory or defeat he was the soul of good cheer. His mellow musical voice could be heard above the din of battle singing,

> "If you want to have a good time
> Jine the cavalry."

Once General Longstreet laughingly ordered General Stuart to leave camp, saying he made the cavalryman's life seem so attractive that all the infantrymen wanted to desert and "jine the cavalry."

On December 20, 1861, while the army was in winter quarters at Manassas, Stuart was placed in command of about 1,500 infantry, a battery of artillery, and a small body of cavalry, for the purpose of covering the movements of General J. E. Johnston's wagon train which had been sent to procure forage for the Confederate troops. It was most important this wagon train should be protected and the pickets had advanced to Dranesville with the cavalry following closely, when a Federal force of nearly 4,000 men, supported by two other brigades, attacked the pickets. The pickets were driven back, and the Federal artillery and infantry occupied the town, where they posted themselves in a favorable position.

Stuart, when informed the Federals held the town, sent at once to recall the wagons and advanced as quickly as possible with the rest of his force to engage the Federals while the wagons were gaining a place of safety. The Federals had a much larger force of infantry and had a good position for their artillery; so Stuart, after two hours of unequal combat, was forced to retire with heavy loss in killed and wounded. The wagons, however, were saved from capture; and the next morning when Stuart returned to renew the attack, he found that the Federals had retired.

In this battle of Dranesville, the Confederate loss was nearly 200 and that of the Federals was only 68. This was the first serious check Stuart had received, but he had displayed so much prudence and skill in extricating the wagons and his small force from the sudden danger that he retained the entire confidence of his men.

Writing about this battle to his wife, Stuart said, "The enemy's force was at least four times larger than mine. Never was I in greater personal danger. Horses and men fell about me like tenpins, but thanks to God neither I nor my horse was touched."

In the meanwhile, the Federal commander, General McClellan, had been organizing his forces and by March, 1862, he had under him in front of Washington a large army splendidly armed and equipped. General Johnston had too small an army to engage the Federal hosts; and so late in March he fell back from Manassas and encamped on the south side of the Rappahannock river.

General McClellan moved his large army to Fortress Monroe, and it was then seen that he intended to advance to Richmond by way of the Peninsula, — that is, the portion of tidewater Virginia lying between the James and York rivers.

The brave Confederate general, Magruder, stationed at Yorktown, was joined by General Johnston with his whole army. They saw, however, it would be impossible to hold that position against McClellan, and so the Confederates gave up the town and retired toward Richmond.

The cavalry under Stuart skillfully guarded the rear of the army and concealed its movements from the Federals. At Williamsburg a stubborn and brilliant battle was fought, in which Johnston's rear guard repelled the Federals. After the battle, the cavalry and the Stuart Horse Artillery protected the rear of the Confederate army as it withdrew toward Richmond and screened the infantry as it took position along the southern bank of the Chickahominy River.

McClellan placed his army on the north bank of the same river, and on May 31 and June 1, he threw a large force across the river and engaged the army of Johnston in the battle of Seven Pines. This battle was only a partial victory for the Confederates, and as the river was bordered by wide marshes and dense woods, neither side could make use of cavalry in the conflict. General Stuart, however, was actively engaged in giving personal assistance to General Longstreet on the field.

In his report of the battle. General Longstreet said: "Brigadier J. E. B. Stuart, in the absence of any opportunity to use his cavalry, was of material service by his presence with me on the field."

In this battle of Seven Pines, General Johnston was severely wounded and gave place to General R. E. Lee, who was thus put in command of the army defending Richmond and of all of the other Confederate forces in Virginia. McClellan's magnificent army, now numbering 115,000 men, stretched from Meadow Bridge on the right to the Williamsburg Road on the left, having in front the marshes of the Chickahominy as natural barriers. By entrenching his army behind positions which he secured from time to time, he advanced until at one point he was only five miles from Richmond and could see the spires of the churches and hear the bells ringing for services.

General Lee had a much smaller army with which to repel this large entrenched army and he withdrew to the south side of the Chickahominy. It was very important to him to learn the position and strength of the Union forces, so he might be able to attack them at the weakest point. In order to gain this information, he resolved to send General Stuart with 1,200 cavalry to make a raid toward the White House on the Pamunkey River, which was the base of supplies for the Federal troops. General Lee wrote to General Stuart, giving definite instructions about this scouting expedition.

The letter said: "You are desired to make a scout movement, to the rear of the enemy now posted on the Chickahominy River, with a view of gaining intelligence of his operations, communications, etc., of driving in his foraging parties, and securing such grain and cattle for ourselves as you can make arrangements to have driven in.

"Another object is to destroy his wagon trains said to be daily passing from the Piping-Tree road to his camp on the Chickahominy. The utmost vigilance on your part will be necessary to prevent any surprise to yourself, and the greatest caution must be practiced in keeping well in your front and flanks reliable scouts to give you information.

"You will return as soon as the object of your expedition is accomplished, and you must bear in mind while endeavoring to execute the general purpose of your mission, not to hazard unnecessarily your command. Be content to accomplish all the good you can, without feeling it necessary to obtain all that might be desired."

Such a raid demanded great daring and skill, coupled with cool judgment, and General Lee knew these qualities were possessed by the man to whom he entrusted this responsible and dangerous undertaking. As we are to see, Stuart carried out his instructions in an able and brilliant manner and accomplished even more than was hoped by General Lee.

In the first place, Stuart chose for the enterprise men and horses picked to stand the strain of rapid movement. Colonel Fitzhugh Lee, Colonel W. H. F. Lee, and Colonel W. T. Martin were in command of the cavalry and Colonel James Breathed commanded the one battery of artillery.

Early on the morning of June 12, Stuart and his chosen troopers started on the famous "Chickahominy Raid," or "Pamunkey Expedition" as it is sometimes called. In order to mask his real purpose, Stuart marched directly northward twenty-two miles. At sunrise the next morning, the little band of horsemen mounted and turned abruptly eastward toward Hanover Courthouse. They found the town in possession of a body of Federal cavalry which retired as the Confederate troopers advanced. The Confederates then passed on without serious trouble as far as Totopotomy Creek. Here, however, Stuart's advance guard was attacked by a company of Federal troopers. Finding themselves outnumbered and almost surrounded, these troopers retired to the main body of Federal troops commanded by Captain Royall, who at once drew up his forces to receive the attack. Stuart immediately ordered a squadron to charge with sabers, in columns of fours. Captain Latané, a gallant young officer, who was that day commanding the squadron, met Captain Royall in a hand-to-hand en- counter. Roy all was seriously wounded by a thrust from Latané's saber. Latané fell dead, pierced by a bullet from Royall's pistol. The Federals fled in dismay, but soon rallied and returned to the charge, only to be again repulsed, whereupon they retired to the Union lines.

Fitz Lee learned from some of the prisoners that the Federal camp was not far away and, having obtained from Stuart permission to pursue the Union troops, he pushed on to Old Church, repelled the cavalry, and destroyed the camp.

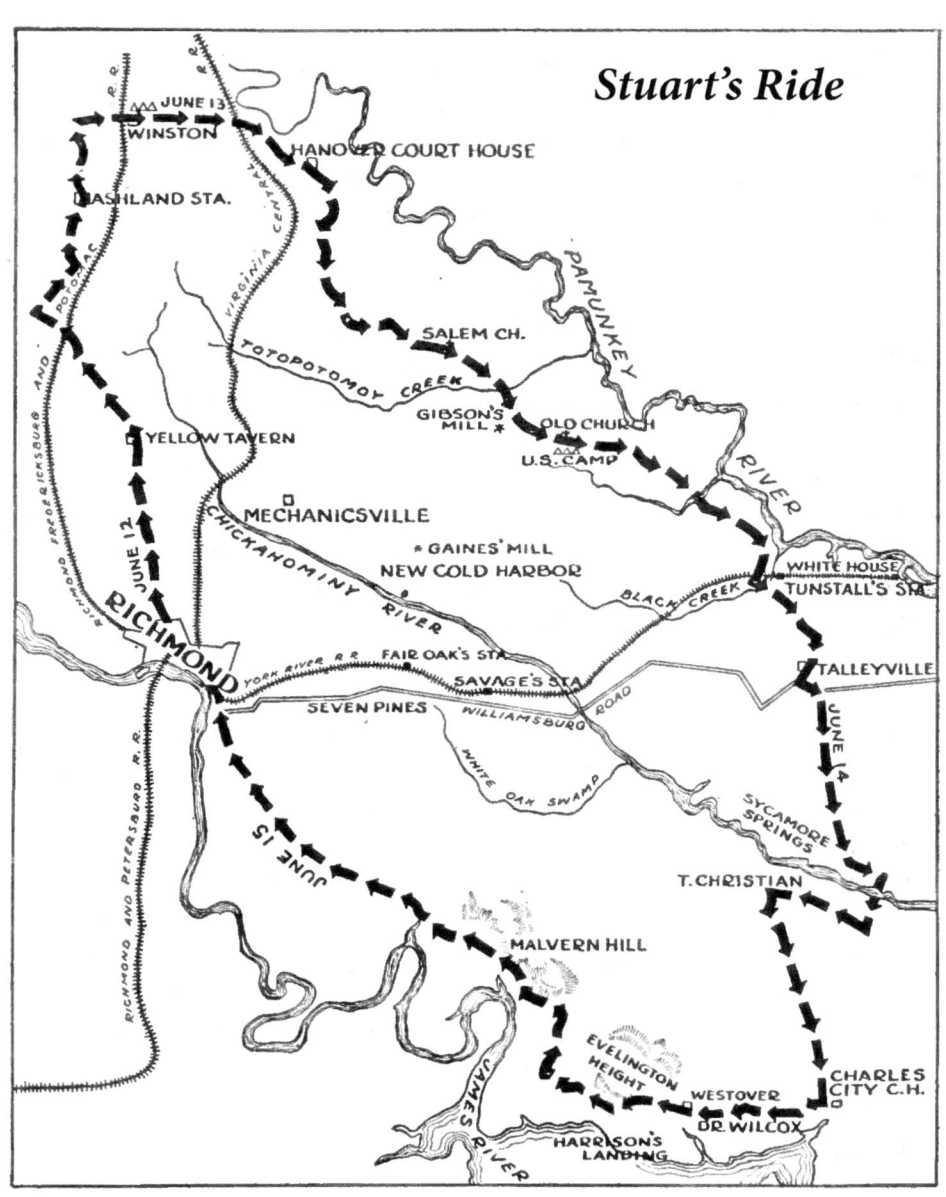

General Stuart had now carried out the chief order given by General Lee, — that is, he had ridden to the rear of McClellan's army and had discovered the Federal right wing did not extend toward the railway and Hanover Courthouse — but it was a vexing problem how to bring this valuable information to his commanding general. The route the young officer had just passed was doubtless by this time swarming with Federals. The best way to return to Richmond would probably be to ride quickly around the entire Federal army and cross the Chickahominy River to the left of McClellan, before troops were sent to cut him off. Without halting or consulting with any of his officers, Stuart decided there was less risk in following this circuitous route, especially as he had with him for a guide Lieutenant James Christian whose home was on the Chickahominy and who said that the command could safely cross a private ford on his farm.

The Federals were under the impression there was a very large force of Confederates on the raid; and so they were collecting infantry and cavalry at Totopotomy Bridge to cut off the return of the raiders. Stuart, however, passed on toward Tunstall's Station, on the York River Railroad, four miles from the White House which was the principal supply station of the Federal army.

He now proceeded to carry out the second part of Lee's instructions, — namely, to destroy whatever supplies he might find on the way. As he passed on, numbers of wagons fell into his hands. He sent two squadrons to Putney's Ferry and burned two large transports and numbers of wagons laden with supplies. Approaching Tunstall's Station, one of the supply depots of the Federals, he sent forward a body of picked men to cut the telegraph wires and obstruct the railroad. Before they could perform the latter task, a train approached bearing soldiers and supplies to McClellan's army. The Confederates fired on it, but instead of stopping the brave engineer stood at his post and carried the train by at full speed. He was struck by a shot and fell dying at his post, while the Confederates gave a cheer for his courage in risking his life to save his charge from their hands.

Vast quantities of Federal stores were destroyed by the Confederates whose men and horses reveled in an unusual supply of good rations and provender. It was now nearly dark and Stuart's position was exceedingly dangerous. Behind him were regiments of cavalry in hot pursuit. Not more than four or five miles distant were the entrenchments of McClellan, whence in a short time troops could be sent by rail to cut off his progress to the James river. Before him was the Chickahominy now a raging torrent from the spring rains. His chief guides through this maze of swamps and forest roads were Private Richard Frayser and Lieutenant Christian whose homes were near and who knew every part of the country through which they were passing. Stuart had the advantage also of knowing from his scouts just where the enemy was located.

Having formed his plans, swiftness and boldness were his watchwords. After he had destroyed the Federal supplies at Tunstall's Station and burned the railroad bridge over Black Creek, he set out about dark for Talleysville, four miles distant, where he halted for three hours and a half, in order to allow men and horses to rest and scattered troopers to come up.

Colonel John S. Mosby, later one of Stuart's chief scouts, was at that time his aide. In describing the raid, Mosby said one who had never taken part in such an expedition could form no idea of the careless gayety of the men that night. When they had set out the day before, they did not know where they were going. Now they were aware they were riding around McClellan and the boldness of the movement fired their imaginations, quickened their pulses, and roused their courage to any deed of daring. Therefore, in the midst of danger, they sang and laughed and feasted; and at midnight when the bugle sounded "Boots and Saddles," every horseman was ready for whatever might come.

At daybreak on June 14, the Confederates reached the ford on Sycamore Springs, Christian's farm, — a ford no longer for the river swollen by the heavy rains had overflowed its banks and become a raging torrent. Colonel Lee and a few men swam their horses across the stream and back again; but it was evident the weaker horses and the artillery could not cross at that point. The Confederates then cut down trees tall enough to span the stream, and attempted to build a rough bridge, but the trees were swept down the rapid current as soon as they touched the water.

Stuart rode up and sat on his horse, calmly stroking his long silken beard as he watched his cavalryman's bootless efforts. Every other face betrayed keen anxiety. Learning there was the remains of an old bridge a few miles below, he moved the command thither with all speed. A deserted warehouse was near the old bridge, and a large force of men was set at work to tear down the house in order to secure material to rebuild the bridge. While the work was going on, Stuart laughed and jested with his officers.

The Chickahominy River

The men worked with such swiftness that within three hours the bridge was ready for the cavalry and artillery to pass over; and at one o'clock that afternoon, the whole command had crossed. During those hours of anxiety, Fitz Lee, in command of the rear guard, had driven off several parties of Federal Cavalry. After all the Confederates gained the southern shore — Fitz Lee being the last man to cross — the bridge was burned to prevent pursuit. The men were exultant and happy at having crossed the river, but they were by no means out of danger, being thirty-five miles from Richmond and still far within the lines of McClellan. Stuart, who knew every moment was precious to General Lee, hastened on at sunset with only one courier and his trusty guide Frayser and arrived at Richmond about sunrise on the morning of June 15. The men rested several hours and then were led by Colonel Fitz Lee safely back to their own camp where they were greeted with enthusiastic cheers by their comrades.

As soon as General Stuart reached Richmond, he sent Frayser to inform Mrs. Stuart of his safe return, while he himself rode to General Lee's headquarters with his wonderful report.

The burial of Latané.

He had been sent to find out the position of the right wing of McClellan's army. He had not only located that, but he had destroyed a large amount of United States property, brought off one hundred and sixty-five prisoners and two hundred and sixty horses and mules. With only twelve hundred men, he had ridden around the great Federal army — a distance of about ninety miles in about fifty-six hours — with the loss of only one man, the lamented young Latané. By that dashing ride, Stuart gained for himself world-wide fame and an honorable place among the great cavalry leaders of all time. The Chickahominy Raid was one of the most brilliant cavalry achievements in history, and it inspired the Confederates with fresh courage and excited Federal dread of the bold cavalrymen who attempted and accomplished seemingly impossible things.

The information gained was invaluable for it made it possible for General Lee to send Jackson against the right flank of McClellan and to defeat the Federals at Cold Harbor.

In the Seven Days' Battle around Richmond, which began on June 26, Stuart at first guarded the left of Jackson's march. In the battle of Gaines's Mill, he found a suitable position for the artillery. He sent forward two guns under Pelham, a gallant young gunner from Alabama, who kept up an unequal combat for hours with two Federal batteries. When the Federal lines had been forced at Gaines's Mill and Cold Harbor, Stuart advanced three miles to the left; but finding no trace of the Federals, he returned that night to Cold Harbor. On June 28, he proceeded toward the White House on the Pamimkey River, which the Federals had abandoned and burned. They had also set fire to many valuable stores and munitions of war. The illustration on the next page is from a war-time photograph, showing the railroad bridge across the Pamunkey River which was destroyed in order to render the road useless to the Confederates. When McClellan changed his base from the White House to James river, he had two trains loaded with food and ammunition run at full speed off the embankment in the left foreground into the river, in order to keep these stores from falling into the hands of the Southern troops.

An interesting account of this campaign is given by Heros Von Borcke. Von Borcke was a noble young Prussian officer who gave his services as a volunteer to the Confederacy, just as LaFayette had given his services to the Colonies in the War of the Revolution; Von Borcke served the South so loyally that near the close of the war the Confederate Con-

Ruins of the railroad bridge across the Pamunkey River.

gress drew up a resolution of thanks for his services in just the same form that the Colonies had thanked LaFayette.

Von Borcke was one of Stuart's aides and he distinguished himself by his gallantry during the Chickahominy raid. He tells us that when the Confederates arrived at the White House they found burning pyramids built of barrels of eggs, bacon and hams, and barrels of sugar. There were also boxes of oranges and lemons and other luxuries. Many of these luxuries were rescued by the Confederates, and when Von Borcke reached the plantation, shortly after it had been taken, he found General Stuart seated under a tree drinking a big glass of iced lemonade, an unusual treat for a Confederate soldier. All of Stuart's troops had such a feast as was seldom enjoyed during the war, and large quantities of supplies and equipments were forwarded to the Confederate quartermaster at Richmond.

The Federal gunboat, *Marhlehead*, was still in sight on the river. The soldiers at that period had an almost superstitious fear of the bombs thrown by the big guns of the gunboats, which made an awful whizzing noise and burst into many fragments. Stuart decided he would teach his troopers a lesson and show them how little harm the dreaded shells did at short range. He selected seventy-five men whom he armed with carbines and placed under command of Colonel W. H. F. Lee who led them down to the landing. They fired at the boat and skirmishers were sent ashore from the boat to meet them. A brisk skirmish followed, during which Stuart brought up one gun of Pelham's battery. This threw shells upon the decks of the *Marblehead*, while the screeching bombs of the big guns of the boat went over the heads of Pelham's battery, far away into the depths of the swamps. The skirmishers hurried back to the *Marblehead*, and it steamed away down the river, pursued as far as possible by shells from Pelham's plucky little howitzer.

Stuart sent General Lee the important news that McClellan was seeking a base upon the James river, and then stayed the remainder of the day at the White House where he found enough undestroyed provisions to satisfy the hunger of the men and horses of his command.

After severe engagements with the Confederates at Savage Station and Frayser's Farm, the Union forces were forced to retreat, closely followed by Jackson and Stuart. On the evening of July 1, was fought the bloody battle of Malvern Hill, after which McClellan retreated by night down the James to Harrison's Landing where he was protected by the gunboats.

Early on the morning of July 2, Stuart started in pursuit and found the Federals in position at Westover. The next day he took possession of Evelington Heights, a tableland overlooking McClellan's encampment and protecting his line of retreat. Here Stuart expected to be supported by Longstreet and Jackson, and he opened fire with Pelham's howitzer.

The Federal infantry and artillery at once moved forward to storm the heights. Jackson and Longstreet were delayed by terrific storms, and Stuart unsupported held his position until two o'clock in the afternoon when his ammunition gave out. He then retired and joined the main body of the infantry, which did not arrive until after the Federals had taken possession of Evelington Heights and were fortifying it strongly.

The two armies now had a breathing spell of about one month. McClellan's defeated hosts remained in their protected position at Harrison's Landing until the middle of August, when they were recalled to join General Pope at Manassas. General Lee's army was withdrawn nearer to Richmond which was saved from immediate danger.

General Stuart in 1862.

CHAPTER V
A MAJOR GENERAL: CAMP LIFE AND THE SECOND BATTLE OF MANASSAS
1862

As a reward for his faithful and efficient services in the Peninsular Campaign, Stuart received his commission as major general of cavalry on July 25, 1862. His forces were now organized into two brigades, with Brigadier General Wade Hampton in command of the first and Brigadier General Fitzhugh Lee in command of the second. During the month following the defeat of McClellan, these two brigades were placed by turns on picket duty on the Charles City road to guard Richmond and in the camp of instruction at Hanover Courthouse.

While conducting this camp of instruction where he drilled his men in the cavalry tactics which were later to win them such honor, Stuart and his staff were often pleasantly entertained at neighboring plantations. Mrs. Stuart with her two little children. Flora, five years of age, and Jimmy aged two was able to be near the general once more. The time passed pleasantly, enlivened by cavalry drills, visits from the young officers to the ladies of the vicinity, serenades and dances, and visits from the ladies to the general's headquarters.

One Sunday evening as the general and most of his staff were visiting at Dundee, the plantation near which their camp was situated, a stable in the yard caught fire and the visitors proved themselves as good firemen as they were soldiers. The young Prussian officer, Von Borcke, an unusually large and heavily-built man, was so energetic in his efforts, that after the fire was out, the general, who was always fond of a joke, insisted he had seen the young officer rush from the burning building with a mule under one arm and two little pigs under the other.

Stuart was soon called away from this pleasant life to make an inspection of all the Confederate cavalry forces. It was evident General Lee's army would soon be engaged against a new Federal commander. General Pope, who was concentrating a large army on the Rapidan river. General

Life of General J. E. B. Stuart

Jackson, who had been sent to hold General Pope in check, had his headquarters at Gordonsville.

Major Von Borcke tells us the cars carrying the Confederate troops to Gordonsville were so crowded that General Stuart rode on the tender of the engine, rather than take a seat away from one of the soldiers. It was a hot night in July and there was a dense smoke from the engine, but it was so dark it was not until they reached Gordonsville the general discovered both Von Borcke and himself were so black with soot that their best friends would not have recognized them. Indeed, it took a great deal of soap and water to make them presentable once more.

Stuart reached Jackson's headquarters on August 10, the day after the Federal advance guard had been defeated in the battle of Cedar Run. At Jackson's request, Stuart took command of a reconnaissance to find out the position and strength of the enemy. Upon hearing his report, Jackson decided to remain for the present on the defensive.

In the meantime. General Lee, who was watching General McClellan's army still encamped at Harrison's Landing, received information the latter had been ordered to withdraw his forces and join General Pope at Manassas.

Leaving a small force in front of Richmond, Lee hastened to join Jackson so they could engage Pope before his already large army was reinforced by McClellan. The cavalry was kept very busy at this time as it was necessary to defend the Central Road, now the Chesapeake and Ohio, from Federal raids.

On the night of August 17, Stuart himself barely escaped capture. He wrote an interesting account of this adventure to his wife, and Mrs. Stuart has kindly allowed us to use the letter in this book. Here it is:

Rapidan Valley, August 19, 1862.
My Dear Wife — I had a very narrow escape yesterday morning. I had made arrangement for Lee's Brigade to move across from Davenport's bridge to Raccoon ford where I was to meet it, but Lee went by Louisa Court House. His dispatch informing me of the fact did not reach me, consequently I went down the Plank road to the place of rendezvous. Hearing nothing of him, I stopped for the night and sent Major Fitzhugh with a guide across to meet General Lee. At sunrise yesterday a large body of cavalry from the very direction from which Lee was expected, approached crossing the Plank road just below me and going directly to-

wards Raccoon Ford. Of course I thought it was Lee — as no Yankees had been seen about for a month, hut as a measure of prudence I sent down two men to ascertain. They had not gone 100 yards before they were fired on and pursued rapidly by a squadron.

I was in the yard bareheaded, my hat being in the porch. I just had time to mount my horse and clear the back fence, having no time to get my hat or anything else. I lost my haversack, blanket, talma, cloak, and *hat*, with that *palmetto star* — too bad, wasn't it? I am all right again, however, and I am greeted, on all sides with congratulations and "w*hereas your hat!*" I intend to make the Yankees pay for that hat.

Poor Fitzhugh was not so fortunate. He was captured four miles off under similar circumstances, with his fine grey. He will be exchanged in ten days, however. Von Borcke and Dabney were with me (five altogether) and their escape was equally miraculous. Dundee is the best place for you at present. We will have hot work I think tomorrow. My cavalry has an important part to play.

Love to all, my two sweethearts included.
God bless you.

J. E. B. Stuart.

A few days later, as you will hear, General Stuart collected payment for his lost hat from General Pope himself. But before this took place, the Confederate cavalry was engaged in several skirmishes with the Federals. There was a severe encounter at Brandy Station on August 20 when sixty-five prisoners were captured. The regiments which had fought under Ashby, a gallant young officer who had been killed in the Valley, were now added to Stuart's division as Robertson's Brigade. At Brandy Station, these troopers fought under Stuart for the first time and he was much pleased at their dash and bravery.

While Lee, who had now joined Jackson, was waiting a favorable opportunity to attack the Federals, Stuart begged permission to pass to the rear of Pope's army and cut his line of communication at Catlett's Station where there was a large depot of supplies. General Lee gave his consent, and on the morning of August 22, General Stuart crossed the Rappahannock at Waterloo Bridge, to make a second raid to the rear of the Federal army.

By nightfall the Confederates reached Auburn near Catlett's Station, where they captured the Federal pickets. Just as they reached the station, however, a violent storm arose; and amid the wind and the rain and the

Catlett Station where Stuart made a raid and captured Pope's baggage, A.R.Waud

darkness, it seemed impossible to find their way. Fortunately, they captured a negro who knew Stuart and who offered to show them the way to Pope's headquarters. They accepted his guidance and soon the Confederate cavalry surprised the unsuspecting enemy, attacked the camp, and captured a number of officers belonging to Pope's staff, as well as his horses, baggage, a large sum of money, and his dispatch book which contained copies of the letters he had written to the government, telling the location and plans of his army. But for the fact that General Pope was out on a tour of inspection, he himself would have been captured.

In the meantime, two of Stuart's regiments had gained another part of the camp, and an attempt was made to destroy the railroad bridge over Cedar Run. But on account of the heavy rain it was impossible to fire it, and, in the dense darkness, it was equally hard to cut asunder the heavy timbers with the few axes which they found. Therefore, with more than three hundred prisoners and valuable spoils, Stuart retired before daybreak and regained in safety the Confederate lines.

Major Von Borcke gives an interesting incident of their return march. As the troops — wet, cold, and hungry — passed through Warrenton, coffee was served them by a number of young girls. One of the girls recognized among the prisoners General Pope's quartermaster. He had boasted several days before, when at her father's house, that he would enter Richmond within a month. She had promptly bet him a bottle of wine he would not be able to do it, but as he was now a prisoner he would be obliged to enter the city even earlier than he had hoped. She, therefore, asked General Stuart's permission to offer the quartermaster a bottle of wine from his own captured supplies. The general readily granted her request, and the Yankee prisoner entered good-naturedly into the jest, saying he would always be willing to drink the health of so charming a person.

In retaliation for the loss of his hat and cloak, General Stuart sent General Pope's uniform to Richmond where for some days it hung in one of the shop windows, to the delight of the populace who especially disliked Pope on account of his bombast and cruelty. He had boasted he had come from the West where his soldiers always saw the backs of their enemies, and he had authorized his soldiers to take whatever they wished from the citizens of Virginia, whom he held responsible for damage done by raiding parties of the Confederate army.

Life of General J. E. B. Stuart

Two weeks later, General Stuart wrote his wife that Parson Landstreet, a member of his staff who had been captured by the Federals, brought him a message from General Pope. Pope said that he would send back Stuart's hat if Stuart would return his coat.

"But," wrote Stuart, "1 have got to see my hat first."

It was against General Pope the second Battle of Manassas was fought, August 28, 29 and 30, 1862. General Stuart and his cavalry in the maneuvers preceding the battle, screened the flank march of Jackson's troops to Grovetown, by which movement they placed themselves between the Federal rear and Washington. It took two days for Jackson's "foot cavalry" to make this march, and so perfectly did Stuart do his work that as late as August 28, Pope did not know to what place Jackson had marched from Manassas.

In the three days' battle which followed, the cavalry was ever on the flank of the army, observing the Federals and guarding against attacks. On the morning of August 29, after a sharp skirmish, Stuart met Lee and Longstreet and opened the way for them to advance to the support of Jackson whose forces on the right wing were engaged in unequal and critical combat. Later on the same day, Stuart saw the Federals were massing in front of Jackson, and with a small detachment of cavalry aided by Pelham and his guns, he gallantly held large forces in check and protected Jackson's captured wagon train of supplies. On the afternoon of August 30, the cavalry did most effectual service, following the retreating Federals and protecting the exposed Confederate flank against heavy cavalry attacks. During the engagements, the Confederate infantry could not have held its position but for the assistance of the cavalry under the able direction of Stuart.

In these battles, Pope had forces largely superior in number and equipment to Lee's, but Pope's losses in killed and wounded were much the heavier. Finally he was forced to retreat toward Washington, leaving in the hands of the Confederates many prisoners as well as captured artillery, arms, and a large amount of stores. The North seemed panic-stricken, as Washington was now directly exposed to the attacks of the Confederates.

CHAPTER VI
THE MARYLAND CAMPAIGN 1862

General Lee knew, however, that he did not have men enough to take by assault the strong fortifications around Washington, and he, therefore, planned to cross over into Maryland before the Federal army had recovered from its defeat, when its commanders were least expect- him. In order that he might completely mislead them and make it appear he was beginning a general attack on Washington, he ordered Stuart and his troops to advance toward that city.

In their advance, they engaged in several sharp skirmishes with the Federals, finally driving them from Fairfax Courthouse, where, amid the cheers of the inhabitants, Major Von Borcke planted the beloved Confederate flag on a little common in the center of the village.

The people of this section had been under Federal control for several months and their joy at seeing Stuart and his troops was unbounded. They flocked to the roadside to get a glimpse of the great cavalry leader.

One lady, who had lost two sons in battle, came forward as the troops passed her home and asked permission to kiss the general's battle flag. She held by the hand her only surviving son, a lad of fifteen years, and declared herself ready if it were needed to give his life too for her country.

On September 5, General Stuart and his forces crossed the Potomac. Four days later, General Lee moved his entire army across the river, encamped at Frederick, Maryland, and sent General Jackson to capture the strongly fortified Federal arsenal at Harper's Ferry.

Major Von Borcke, from whose *Memoirs of the Confederate War for Independence* we shall borrow several interesting incidents of this Maryland campaign, tells us the crossing of the cavalry at White's Ford was one of the most picturesque scenes of the war. The river is very wide at this point, and its steep banks, rising to the height of sixty feet, are overshadowed by large trees that trail from their branches a perfect network of graceful and luxuriant vines. A sandy island about midstream broke the passage of the horsemen and artillery, and as a column of a thousand troops passed over, the rays of the setting sun made the water look like burnished gold. The hearts of the soldiers crossing the river thrilled at the sound of the familiar and inspiring strains of *Maryland, my Maryland* which greeted them from the northern bank.

Major Heros Von Borcke

The enthusiasm of the Maryland people at Poolesville, where Stuart first stopped, was boundless. Two young merchants of the village suddenly resolved to enlist in the cavalry and they put up all their goods at auction. The soldiers with the eagerness and carelessness of children cleared out both establishments in less than an hour. Many other recruits were made in this village, all the young men seeming to feel the inspiration of General Stuart's favorite song,

> "If you want to have a good time
> Jine the cavalry."

At Urbana, a pretty little village on the road to Frederick, where General Stuart with one division of his forces camped for several days, a most exciting ball was held on the evening of September 8. There were many charming families living in the neighborhood, and General Stuart and his staff decided to give a dance at an old, unused academy located on a hill just outside of the town. The young ladies of the neighborhood willingly lent their help, and evening found the halls of the academy lighted by tallow candles and draped with garlands of roses and with battle flags borrowed from the regiments of the brigades. Music was furnished by the band of a Mississippi regiment. The ball, which had opened to the rousing strains of *Dixie*, was at its height, when a young orderly rushed in and to the accompaniment of distant shots reported the Federals had driven in the pickets and were attacking the camp.

Wild confusion prevailed. The officers got rapidly to horse and anxious mamas collected their daughters. Upon reaching the scene of action. General Stuart found the danger had been overestimated and the Federals were already beginning to retreat. In a short while, they had been driven back; and by one o'clock, the staff officers had brought the young ladies back to the academy and the ball had a second and more auspicious opening. Dancing continued until dawn, when some soldiers wounded in the skirmish were brought in, and the ball room was soon converted into a hospital and the fair dancers into willing if inexperienced nurses.

The next day, General Fitz Lee's brigade was engaged in a skirmish, and the day following Colonel Munford, who was commanding Robertson's Brigade, had a sharp encounter with Federals at Sugar Loaf Mountain. By Sept. 11, the Federal cavalry was attacking in such force that General Stuart saw it was necessary to order a retreat toward Frederick. General Fitz Lee commanded the advance; Colonel Munford protected the rear, which as it approached Urbana had a sharp skirmish with the closely-following Federal cavalry. General Stuart and his staff, however, did not tear themselves away from their friends in this hospitable little village until the Union troops were within half a mile of the place and several shells had exploded in the street. From Urbana the cavalry went to Frederick. Many years after the war was over, Mrs. Stuart received a letter from a New York physician, who at the time of the Maryland campaign had just won his title and a position on the staff of one of the Union hospitals in Frederick.

He told about meeting General Stuart and then said, "1 wish to bear testimony to the fact that not only myself, but all the friends of the Union cause in Frederick, so far as I could learn, were kindly treated by both officers and private soldiers. I do not remember of a single instance where private property was molested, nor was any taunt, indignity, or insult offered to any person. Whittier's "Barbara Frietchie" which has attracted so much attention — even that is fiction."

At Frederick, Stuart found General Lee had already retreated across South Mountain and taken a position at Sharpsburg on Antietam Creek, while Jackson was investing Harper's Ferry. Look at the map on page 95 and you will see southwest of Frederick rises a small spur of the Blue Ridge, called Catoctin Mountain on the other side of which is a broad, fertile valley extending for about six miles to the base of South Mountain. On the opposite side of South Mountain is Sharpsburg, and across the same mountain to the south is Harper's Ferry which Jackson had been ordered to capture before he marched north to join Lee and Longstreet at Sharpsburg.

Now you can see until Harper's Ferry fell it was necessary the cavalry should hinder the advance of the Federal army under McClellan until Jackson could join Lee. This was especially difficult, because an order from General Lee to General D. H. Hill, explaining fully the commanding general's plans and the location of all his forces, had fallen into the hands of General McClellan and he was advancing a tremendous army toward Sharpsburg as rapidly as possible.

As General McClellan's forces advanced, General Stuart retreated slowly, contesting every inch of ground. His retreat across Catoctin Mountain was through Braddock's Gap, along the same road where eighty-seven years before, the young patriot, George Washington, had accompanied General Braddock on the fatal expedition against Fort

Duquesne. In this gap, Stuart had a sharp encounter with the Federals. He and Major Von Borcke who was commanding a gun on the height above the pass, narrowly escaped being captured by Federal skirmishers who, under cover of the dense forest, had worked their way around behind the gun.

Another sharp encounter took place on Kittochtan creek at Middletown, half way across the valley, where General Stuart delayed the retreat of his forces so long that they barely escaped capture and reached the foot of South Mountain just in time to protect the two principal passes — Turner's Gap which led directly through Boonsboro to Sharpsburg, and Crampton's Gap which led through Pleasant Valley to Harper's Ferry.

It was necessary to hold these gaps and delay the enemy until Jackson could capture Harper's Ferry and unite his division with the remainder of the army under General Lee. A heavy part of this work fell on the cavalry and the artillery. The retreat of Generals Longstreet and Hill, who had held Turner's Gap until the afternoon of Sept. 14, was covered by General Fitz Lee's brigade which held the Federals in check at every possible point. There was a sharp encounter at Boonsboro, where, in charging, General W. H. F. Lee was ridden down by his own men and narrowly escaped capture.

At Crampton's Gap, which led through Pleasant Valley to Harper's Ferry, Colonel Munford gallantly checked the Federal advance until the evening of Sept. 14, when the troops sent to assist him broke and retreated in bad order through Pleasant Valley. General Stuart had been at Harper's Ferry conferring with General McLaws; when they heard of the engagement at Crampton's Gap, both generals rode quickly forward to meet the routed and panic-stricken troops which they rallied and formed into line of battle. The position they held the next morning was so strong the advancing Federals hesitated to attack; just as the first shots were being exchanged, the news of the surrender of Harper's Ferry caused the attacking party to begin a hasty retreat along the road they had come.

General Stuart at once reported to General Jackson, who requested him to convey the news to General Lee at Sharpsburg. But even now Lee was in great peril. He had with him, on the evening of Sept. 14 when the gaps were stormed, only about 20,000 men; and McClellan's army of more than 87,000 was advancing rapidly to attack him. Lee had now either to recross the Potomac or to fight a battle north of that river.

He decided to make a stand, and on the night of Sept. 14, drew his army across Antietam Creek and took a strong position on a range of hills east of the Hagerstown turnpike. Here he waited for Jackson who, by a forced march, came up in time to take position on the left wing on the morning of September 16. Even when reinforced by Jackson, Lee had a much smaller force than McClellan.

On the evening of Sept. 16, McClellan attacked Jackson's wing at the left of Lee's army, but was repulsed. At early dawn the next day, the attack was renewed and the combat raged all day. When night ended the bloody contest, the Confederates not only held their position, but had advanced their lines on a part of the field. During the entire battle, Stuart with his horse artillery and a small cavalry escort had guarded the open hilly space between Jack- son's left and the Potomac river.

General Jackson in his report of this battle said: "This officer (General Stuart) rendered valuable service throughout the day. His bold use of artillery secured for us an important position which, had the enemy possessed, might have commanded our left."

The next day, Lee waited for McClellan to attack, but no movement came from the hostile camp. Finding out through Stuart's scouts that large bodies of fresh troops were being sent to McClellan, Lee withdrew that night to the south side of the Potomac, and by eleven o'clock the next morning, he was again ready to give battle should the Federals pursue. He had brought off nearly everything of value, leaving behind only several disabled cannon and some of his wounded.

While Fitz Lee's and Munford's troops were left to protect the retreat of the army, Stuart with a small force had gone up the Potomac to Williamsport, hoping to divert the attention of the Federals from the main body of the army and so enable it to cross the river unhindered. This movement was successful, for large Federal forces were sent against him, yet he maintained his position without reinforcements until the night of September 20, when he recrossed the Potomac in safety.

During this short campaign, several interesting incidents occurred. On one occasion, when the Federals were advancing toward Williamsport, a young lady of the town obtained permission to fire a cannon which was about to be discharged. After this, the soldiers always called that cannon "the girl of Williamsport."

Another time. Major Von Borcke tells us he accompanied the general on one of his favorite, yet dangerous reconnoitering expeditions outside of the Confederate lines. They tried to keep themselves concealed by the dense undergrowth, but they must have been observed by the pickets, for in a short while Major Von Borcke heard the "little clicking sound that a saber scabbard often makes in knocking against a tree," and, looking quickly around, he saw a long line of Federal cavalry. A few whispered words to the general were enough; he and his aide put spurs to their horses and once more justified their reputations as expert horsemen, for they were soon hidden by the friendly trees, while their pursuers were firing wildly in vain search for the escaped prey.

There were no serious engagements for the next few weeks and General Lee's army enjoyed a well deserved rest. The cavalry watched the movements of the Federals and protected the camps from alarms. The cavalry headquarters were delightfully situated near Charlestown on the plantation of Mr. A. S. Dandridge. Because of its beautiful grove of huge oak trees, this plantation was called The Bower. A comfortable old brick mansion crowned the summit of a sloping hill on the sides of which the tents of the camp were located under oak trees. At the foot of the hill wound the sparkling little Opequan river. Here provisions were plentiful once more, and the soldiers enjoyed fishing and hunting the small game, — squirrels, rabbits, and partridges — which abounded in the nearby woods.

General Stuart had attached to his staff a remarkable young banjo player, Bob Sweeny, who, with the assistance of two fiddlers and Stuart's mulatto servant Bob who rattled the bones unusually well, furnished music around the camp fire for the men and served also on serenades and at dances given to the officers at the hospitable Dandridge mansion.

General Stuart was very fond of dancing, and when some of the young officers of his staff were occasionally too tired and sleepy to want to join in the fun, he would have them awakened and ordered to attend. Yet they complained that when they did come the general would always get the prettiest girl for his own partner.

But in spite of his joyous, fun-loving disposition, General Stuart was always ready when duty called him. In his book, *Christ in the Camp*, the Rev. J. William Jones says, "Stuart was an humble and earnest Christian who took Christ as his personal Saviour, lived a stainless life, and died a triumphant death."

He tells us General Stuart often came to get his advice in planning services for the soldiers. Once when General Stuart wanted Dr. Jones to recommend a chaplain for the cavalry outposts, the general said, "I do not want a man who is not able to endure hardness as a good soldier. The man who can not endure the hardships and privations of our rough riding and hard service and be in place when needed would be of no earthly use to us and is not wanted at my headquarters."

CHAPTER VII
THE CHAMBERSBURG RAID
1862

On October 8, after a final dance and serenade to the ladies at The Bower, Stuart started out to join the forces that he had ordered to assemble at Darkesville, from which point he was to lead them on the famous "Chambersburg Raid."

The purpose of this raid, which had been ordered by General Lee, was to march into Pennsylvania and Maryland and to secure information concerning the location of McClellan's army, and also to secure provisions and horses for the Confederate forces.

Not a soldier of the 1,800 picked cavalrymen from the brigades of Hampton, Fitz Lee, and Robertson or the gunners under Pelham, knew whither they were going or for what purpose. Most of them, however, had been with Stuart on his Chickahominy Raid, and all were content to follow wherever he led.

In his address to his men at the beginning of the expedition, Stuart said the enterprise on which they were about to start demanded coolness, decision, and bravery, implicit obedience and the strictest order and sobriety in the camp and on the bivouac, but with the hearty cooperation of his officers and men he had no doubt of a success which would reflect credit on them in the highest degree.

The men in fine spirits reached the Potomac after dark. The next morning, they crossed the river at McCoy's Ford, west of McClellan's army which was posted north of the Potomac between Shepherdstown and Harper's Ferry. A heavy fog hung over the river valley and hid them from the Federal infantry which had just passed by.

A signal station on Fairview Heights was taken by twenty men detailed for the purpose and then the column passed on toward Mercersburg. By this time, the Federal pickets were aware of the raid; but as there was no large force of cavalry at hand, its progress was unchecked. On and on the little band of horsemen rode until at nightfall they reached Chambersburg in Pennsylvania. As Maryland was regarded as a Southern State, nothing belonging to its citizens had been disturbed; but when Pennsyl-

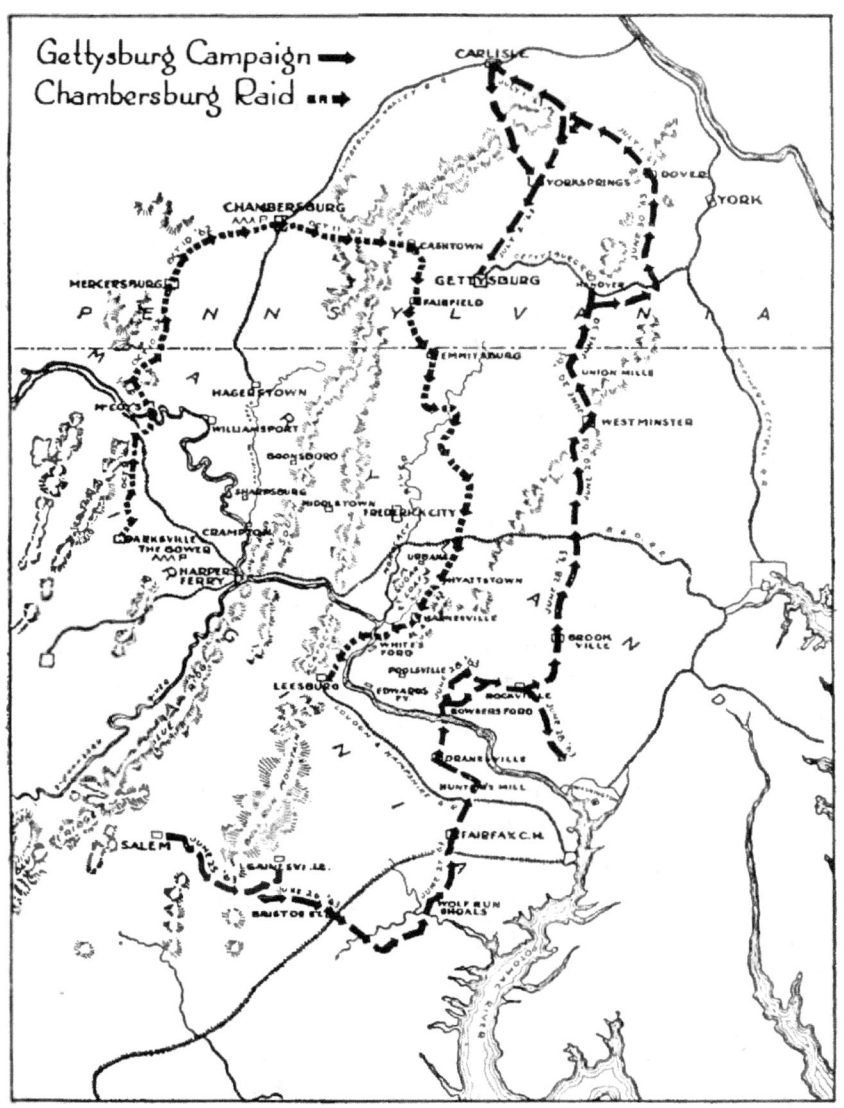

The routes of Stuart's Cavalry in Gettysburg Campaign and Chambersburg Raid.

vania was reached, soldiers detached from the commands for that purpose, seized all suitable horses, giving each owner a receipt, so he could call upon the United States government for payment — thus forcing the administration at Washington either to help equip the Confederate army or to make its own citizens suffer. Stuart, with his usual gallantry, gave orders the men should not take the horses of ladies whom they might meet along the highway.

As the command approached Chambersburg on the night of October 10, a cold drizzling rain set in. Two pieces of artillery were posted so as to command the town, and Lieutenant Thomas Lee with nine men was sent into the town to demand its surrender. No resistance was made and the troops were at once marched into the town and drawn up on the public square. Strict discipline was observed and only Federal property was used or destroyed.

During the night, the rain came down in torrents on the weary, hungry Confederates. Surrounded by increasing dangers, Stuart with his staff neither rested nor slept. By that time, cavalry and infantry were on his track and every ford of the Potomac was strongly guarded. At any time, the heavy rains might cause the river to rise and cut off retreat. His only hope was to move boldly and swiftly to a crossing before the water could descend from the mountains and flood the streams. Stuart decided, however, not to return the way he had come, as large forces of Federal cavalry, like hornets, would be awaiting him there. He resolved to make another ride around McClellan's army and to cross at White's Ford some distance to the east, so close to the Federals that they would not be looking for him there. The very boldness of the plan was its best guarantee of success and the next morning the general started his men on their dangerous march around the enemy.

Colonel A. K. McClure of the *Philadelphia Times*, then a colonel in the Federal army and a resident of Chambersburg, gives the following account of Stuart as he was preparing to leave Chambersburg: "General Stuart sat on his horse in the center of the town, surrounded by his staff, and his command was coming in from the country in large squads, leading their old horses and riding the new ones they had found in the stables hereabout. General Stuart is of medium stature, has a keen eye, and wore immense sandy whiskers and mustache. His demeanor to our people is that of a humane soldier. In several instances his soldiers began to take property from stores, but they were arrested by Stuart's provost guard."

This evidence as to the discipline of Stuart's men comes from a Federal officer, and shows fully the control the general exercised over his command.

The wounded in the Chambersburg hospital were paroled, the telegraph wires were cut, and the ordnance storehouse was blown up by brave Captain M. C. Butler of South Carolina, who now commanded the rear guard. He notified the people near the ordnance storehouse that he was about to set fire to it and then applied a slow fuse. There was a loud explosion and then the flames burst forth. Satisfied that his work was well done. Colonel Butler and his escort set out at a trot to rejoin the command.

On the outskirts of the town, there came galloping up from the rear a young soldier in gray, riding a big black horse. He wore no hat and one boot was gone. He was covered with mud and was soaking wet, for he had come into town with the rear guard about midnight in the darkness and pouring rain. The command had halted for a few hours in a quiet side street and had set out at break of day as the advance guard.

The young soldier's foot had been hurt, so he dismounted and pulled off his boot, in order to ease the pain. He then concluded to lie down for a while and perhaps take a nap, for he was very tired. Tying the bridle rein to his foot, he lay down in the pouring rain and went to sleep. When he awoke, it was broad daylight and he was all alone. In the darkness of the cloudy dawn, his comrades had left him sleeping. His big black horse was still tied to his foot, but his hat, his haversack, and one of his boots were gone. Rising quickly, he mounted his horse and was trying to decide which way to go when an old lady raised a window near by and called out, "Sonny, your folks have gone that way." With a lighter heart he thanked her, and set off at a gallop along the Gettysburg road to which she had pointed. As he sped along, the people called out, "Go it, Johnny! Goodby, Johnny! Hurry, Johnny!" All seemed to be in a good humor over the speedy departure of the Confederates. It was not many minutes before he reached the rear of Butler's detachment, and was safe.

Soon after the break of day, the advance column under General Fitz Lee started towards Gettysburg, but at Cashtown the column turned south toward Emmitsburg in Maryland. When Stuart arrived at the latter place, the people received him with great joy and the young ladies of the town threw flowers at the troops. But in spite of this hearty welcome, the Confederates could not linger, for they learned that a party of Federals in search of them, had passed only a short time before.

Going in a steady trot without halting, Stuart passed on to the woods of Frederick, and captured a courier with a dispatch from the commander of the party sent out to find him. From this dispatch, he learned the arrangements which had been made to capture him, and learned also the Federals did not know just where he was.

Stuart's sword from Confederate Museum in Richmond, VA.

In the meantime, the Federal cavalry was hurrying to overtake him, but Stuart, aware of his extreme danger, aimed straight for the Potomac. His tired men and horses marched all night, and by dawn on October 13, they reached Hyattstown where a few wagons were captured. On the march, Stuart had learned a division of five thousand men was guarding the fords in front of him. Knowing that delay would increase his peril, he hastened on in the direction of Poolesville where a body of Federal cavalry was located.

When within two miles of that town, guided by Captain White who was familiar with the region, he turned abruptly through some woods which concealed his movements and gained the road leading to the river about two miles distant. Hardly had the Confederates entered this road when the advance squadron met the head of the Federal column coming from Poolesville. General Stuart, who was at the head of the squadron, ordered a charge and drove the Federals back upon the main body half a mile away. Thinking that Stuart was aiming to cross the strongly-guarded ford at the mouth of the Monocacy river, the Federals, instead of seizing this favorable opportunity to make an advance and crush the Confederate cavalry, waited for their infantry to come up.

In the meanwhile. General Fitz Lee's sharpshooters leaped from their horses and went forward while one of Pelham's guns was brought up. Under cover of its fire and screened from view by the ridge upon which it was placed, General Lee's command moved on by a farm road to White's Ford.

When General Lee reached White's Ford, he found a force of two hundred Federal infantry so strongly posted on the steep bank overlooking the ford that a crossing seemed impossible. Infantry in front and cavalry in the rear! Would it be possible to escape from the snare by which they were surrounded? Nothing but boldness and swiftness could save them. General Lee sent a courier to General Stuart who was on the Poolesville road with Pelham's guns and the skirmishers keeping back Federal troopers until the rear guard should come up.

"I do not believe that the ford can be crossed" said General Lee.

Stuart replied, "I am occupied in the rear, but the ford must be crossed at all hazards."

General Lee, therefore, prepared to attack the Federal infantry in its strong position on the bluff One part of his force was to assail it in front and on the left flank, while a strong body of cavalry endeavored to cross and hold the ford. Lee hoped to be able to get one gun placed on the opposite bank and then to fire on the Federal rear.

While making his hurried preparations, it occurred to General Lee to try a game of "bluff." Under flag of truce, he sent a note to the Federal commander, saying General Stuart's whole command was in his front and needless bloodshed would be avoided if he would surrender. Fifteen minutes was allowed him to consider this demand.

After fifteen minutes' anxious waiting and no reply, General Fitz Lee opened with his artillery and was preparing to advance his horsemen, when it was seen that the Federals, with flags flying and band playing, were retreating in perfect order down the river.

A wild cheer broke from the Confederates as some of their men rushed across the ford to place a piece of artillery at the top of the steep bank on the Virginia side of the Potomac. Another gun was hurried forward and placed so as to sweep the tow-path and the approaches to the ford, while the long line of cavalrymen and captured horses passed rapidly across to safety. Once more Stuart had slipped through the hands of his enemy.

In the meanwhile, Pelham held the Federals in check until all but the rear guard under Colonel Butler had passed. Then he began to withdraw, making his last stand on the Maryland side of the ford, where he fired up and down the river at the Federal cavalry now advancing in both directions. But the rear guard was still far behind. Major McClellan tells us General Stuart had sent back four couriers to hurry up Colonel Butler; still he did not come. In this dilemma, Captain Blackford volunteered to find him.

Stuart paused a moment and then extending his hand said, "All right! and if we do not meet again, good-by, old fellow."

Blackford galloped off and found Butler with his own regiment and the North Carolina detachment and one gun, engaged in delaying the advance of the enemy in the Poolesville Road. Blackford rode rapidly

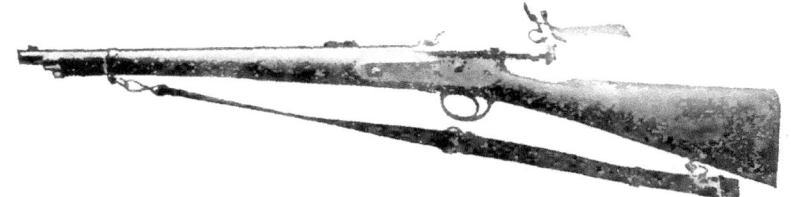

Stuart's carbine from original in Confederate Museum, Richmond, VA.

toward him and shouted, "General Stuart says, 'Withdraw at a gallop, or you will be cut off.'"

"But," replied Butler, with great coolness, "I don't think I can bring off that gun. The horses can't move it."

"Leave the gun and save your men!" replied Blackford.

"Well, we'll see what can be done," said Butler, and then he ordered the drivers to make one more effort. That time they were successful. The weary horses pulled the wheels out of the mudhole and the gun went rattling down the road, followed by the tardy but gallant rear guard. The Federal cavalry and artillery were following and infantry was approaching in two directions; but the rear guard slipped through the net, dashed rapidly across the ford, and soon was safe in Virginia.

The joy of the men and their commander at the success of their expedition was unbounded. The Federals were near enough to hear the Confederate cheers that greeted General Stuart as he rode along his lines on the Virginia side.

In the official report of the expedition, Stuart claimed no personal credit, but closed the report by saying, "Believing that the hand of God was clearly manifested in the deliverance of my command from danger and the crowning success attending it, I ascribe to him the praise, the honor, and the glory."

The march of the Confederate cavalry from Chambersburg is one of the most remarkable in history. In thirty-six hours, the Confederates rode ninety miles, going completely around the Union army. They carried off hundreds of horses, and recrossed the Potomac in the presence of vastly superior forces of the Federals. Only one man was wounded and two stragglers were captured.

General Stuart himself, however, suffered a heavy personal loss, for his servant Bob who rattled the bones so well, got separated from the column, with two of the general's favorite horses, Skylark and Lady Margaret. He wrote his wife he hoped they had fallen into the hands of the good secessionists at Emmitsburg, for he could not bear to think of the Federals having his favorite horses.

The horses of the Federal cavalry had been so worn out in pursuit of the wily Stuart that remounts were necessary before the cavalry could again advance into Virginia. The whole North was astonished and indignant Stuart had again ridden completely around the Union army and had again made his escape.

To the South, Stuart was a peerless hero and he was welcomed with great acclamation. A lady of Baltimore, as a token of her appreciation of his gallantry, sent him a pair of gold spurs. He was very proud of these and in his intimate letters after this, he sometimes signed himself, "K. G. S." or "Knight of the Golden Spurs."

Stuart's pistol from original in Confederate Museum, Richmond, VA.

CHAPTER VIII
THE CAVALRY AT CULPEPER AND FREDERICKSBURG
1862-'63

The brief space of two days was all the time given to the men and horses of Stuart's command to rest and enjoy life at The Bower, before they were again called out to active service. General McClcllan had sent two large forces of infantry and cavalry across the river to find out whether General Lee's army was still in the Valley or whether it had moved east of the Blue Ridge mountains. After several skirmishes with Stuart's cavalry, these troops retired, convinced Lee was still in the Valley.

On October 26, McClellan crossed the Potomac and the weather continuing fine, he advanced his entire army to begin an autumn campaign against Lee. A week later, his forces began to advance toward Washington, a little village northwest of Culpeper and near the headwaters of the Rappahannock. This position was desirable because it would give an easy route toward Richmond. General Lee, however, sent Longstreet at once with some of the cavalry to head off the Federals at Culpeper, while Jackson was to remain in the Valley and threaten their rear.

In the meantime, Stuart bade a final farewell to his pleasant camp quarters and his friends at the Dandridge mansion. His force fell slowly back toward Culpeper, contesting every inch of ground against the overwhelming numbers of the Federal cavalry. Sharp encounters took place at Union, Middleburg, and Upperville, in which the artillery under Pelham did wonderfully daring and effective work. In these encounters, the Federals lost nearly twice as many men as did the Confederates, but it was impossible for Stuart's small forces to hold any permanent ground against the greatly superior numbers now marching against him.

At Ashby's Gap, General Stuart came near being cut off from his own forces. He had commanded Colonel Rosser to hold this gap while he, accompanied by a few members of his staff, rode across the mountain for a conference with General Jackson. When Stuart returned the next day, after a hard ride over a little-used mountain trail, what was his surprise on reaching a point just above what had been his own camp, to find the place literally swarming with blue-coats.

Rosser had found it necessary to withdraw before the superior numbers of the Federals and his couriers who went to inform Stuart of this fact had missed the general who had returned by a shortcut across the mountain. He and his men were indeed in a serious predicament, and had they not found a mountaineer, who knew the trails on the other side of the mountain, there is no telling when or where General Stuart would have joined his command. He was guided safely to Barber's Cross Roads where his forces had retreated and he made the simple and faithful mountaineer happy with a fifty-dollar note.

On November 10, there was an engagement at Barber's Cross Roads, and the Confederate cavalry was forced to retreat through Orleans and across the Rappahannock at Waterloo Bridge. That night Stuart received the news of the death of his dear little daughter, Flora. For some time he had known of her serious illness, and the doctor had written he must come home if he wished to see her, but he knew his country needed him to hold the Federal cavalry in check.

When the second urgent call reached him on the field of battle near Union, he wrote Mrs. Stuart: "I was at no loss to decide that it was my duty to you and to Flora to remain here. I am entrusted with the conduct of affairs, the issue of which will affect you, her, and the mothers and children of our whole country much more seriously than we can believe.

"If my darling's case is hopeless, there are ten chances to one that I will get to Lynchburg too late; if she is convalescent, why should my presence be necessary? She was sick nine days before I knew it. Let us trust in the good God who has blessed us so much, that He will spare our child to us, but if it should please Him to take her from us, let us bear it with Christian fortitude and resignation."

Major Von Borcke, who opened the telegram telling of the child's death, says that when the general read it he was completely overcome, but he bore his loss most bravely, especially when Mrs. Stuart came to visit him a few days later at Culpeper.

He never forgot his "little darling" and often talked of her to Von Borcke, who says very prettily: "Tight blue flowers recalled her eyes to him; in the glancing sunbeams he caught the golden tinge of her hair, and whenever he saw a child with such eyes and hair he could not help tenderly embracing it. He thought of her on his deathbed, and drawing me to him he whispered, 'My dear friend, I shall soon be with my little Flora again.'"

Yet such a father could put aside his own feelings when he felt that his country needed him. Duty to God and his country were his watchwords, and this high and unselfish sense of duty and patriotism was the foundation of his greatness both as a man and a soldier.

The cavalry fell back from Waterloo Bridge to join Longstreet at Culpeper, but every day it was engaged in sharp skirmishes with the Federal cavalry. In one of these engagements, General Stuart had an amusing experience that narrowly escaped being a serious one. Major Von Borcke tells us while his cavalry was being forced back under a very heavy fire, Stuart in endeavoring to make it hold its position, uselessly but according to his custom, exposed his own person on horseback by riding out of the wood into an open field where he and his aide were excellent targets for their enemies. Von Borcke remonstrated, but the general, who could not bear to have the day go against him, curtly said to his young aide, "If it is too hot for you, you can retire."

Of course. Von Borcke remained in his position at the general's side, but he did shelter himself from the rain of bullets, behind a convenient tree. From this position, a few moments later he saw Stuart raise his hand quickly to his beloved mustache, one half of which had been neatly cut away by a whistling bullet.

As a result of their heavy and continuous marching, the horses of Stuart's troops were in bad condition, many of them having sore tongues and a disease known as "grease heel;" in spite of this and the absence of many men who had gone home to procure fresh horses, the services now rendered by the cavalry were invaluable. General Lee said in his report of this campaign that the vigilance, activity, and courage of the cavalry were conspicuous, and to its assistance was due in a great measure the success of some of the army's most important operations.

While General Lee was awaiting the movements of the Federal army, an event happened which changed the entire aspect of military affairs. General McClellan was removed from command and General Burnside was put in his place. General McClellan had been too slow and cautious to suit the authorities at Washington; so, much to the delight of the Confederate government, this able general was removed just as his campaign had begun.

General Burnside remained at Warrenton ten days in order to reorganize his army into three divisions. Then he began to move his forces toward Fredericksburg on the Rappahannock river. This movement was at once observed by Stuart and reported to General Lee who immediately began to move troops toward Fredericksburg. When Burnside 's forces reached the northern bank of the river, they found the town in Lee's possession and the heights to the south of it crowned by his artillery.

General Lee now ordered General Jackson to come from the Valley to join him. While waiting for this reenforcement, he began to construct earthworks for his artillery and to dig rifle-pits for his infantry on the range of hills extending in a semicircle for five miles south of the river. Here with Hampton guarding the left wing of the army and Stuart the right, the Confederates camped in comparative quiet until early in December.

During this period, there were several heavy snowstorms which the soldiers enjoyed like so many schoolboys. Major Von Borcke tells of a snow battle when several hundred men of McLaws' division charged across a snow-covered plain half a mile wide, on the quarters of Hood's division. Suddenly Hood's whole division, led by its officers with colors flying, advanced against the attacking party which was driven back some distance. Then receiving reinforcements from their own division, the men rallied and threw up entrenchments behind which they made a stand. The air was white with flying snowballs, and the contest waxed hottest just at Stuart's headquarters where he stood on a box and cheered the contestants. Hood's men finally drove their opponents from the snow entrenchments, and would have routed them utterly, had not Anderson's division come up to assist their fleeing comrades. With these reinforcements, McLaws' men suddenly turned and drove Hood's division back home. From these sham battles, the army turned soon to real warfare.

General Burnside had posted guns on Stafford Heights opposite Fredericksburg and on December 10, he shelled the town. Then his splendid army of 116,000 men crossed the river on pontoon bridges, and on the morning of December 13, it stormed Lee's position. The battle raged all day, but the Federals were repulsed at all points and when night closed, the Confederates were still holding their position.

This battle of Fredericksburg offered little opportunity for cavalry charges, but General Fitz Lee kept watch over the fords on the Confederate left, while General W. H. F. Lee was posted on the right. Stuart also remained on the right as it was the weakest part of the line, and was in constant conference with Lee and Jackson.

As the Federals made their first advance against the troops of Jackson at Hamilton's Crossing near the extreme right. Major Pelham of the Stuart Horse Artillery in an exposed position opened a cross fire with one gun and caused them to halt for over an hour. Five Federal batteries opened upon him, but he continued to fire until withdrawn by Stuart.

Both General Lee and General Jackson were on the extreme right and witnessed the wonderful work done by Major Pelham's gun. Both of them in their reports of this battle mentioned the genius and bravery of the young Alabamian.

General Jackson asked General Stuart, "Have you another Pelham, general? If so, I wish that you would give him to me."

Major John Pelham

General Lee expected the battle to be renewed the next morning, but Burnside remained quiet, and, on the night of December 15, in a violent storm of wind and rain, he withdrew to the opposite bank.

It soon became evident Burnside had no intention of renewing the combat, but was preparing to pass the winter on the Stafford hills on the northern side of the river. General Lee's army, therefore, went into winter quarters along the south bank of the Rappahannock. The infantry and artillery built snug log huts, and began, in spite of the want of good rations and warm clothes, to enjoy the rest from marching and fighting.

The cavalry, however, had no rest, for upon its vigilance depended the safety of the army. It observed the Federal movements, watched the fords of the river, and made continual raids to the rear of Burnside 's army.

On December 20, General Stuart set out with 1,800 men under the

Life of General J. E. B. Stuart

command of his tried and true generals, Hampton, Fitz Lee, and W. H. F. Lee, on what is known as the "Dumfries Raid." They were to pass by different routes to the rear of Burnside's army, to cut his line of communication with Washington city, and to destroy all wagons and stores they could not bring off.

Stuart led his forces between various army-posts which guarded the rear of Burnside's army, avoiding the strongest and attacking others which he knew to be weak or ignorant of his approach. He at last marched north to Burke's Station, where his keen sense of humor caused him to play a joke on the authorities at Washington.

He surprised the telegraph operator at the instrument, just as he was receiving a message from headquarters at the capital, telling of measures which were being taken to capture Stuart's command. Having thus gained important information, Stuart put one of his own men in the operator's place and sent a message to Meigs, the quartermaster general at Washington.

"I am much satisfied with the transport of mules lately sent, which I have taken possession of, and request that you send me a fresh supply.
J. E. B. Stuart."

This message produced great consternation in Washington, where the people were as afraid of Stuart and his cavalry as they were of the whole Confederate army.

After thus revealing his whereabouts, Stuart marched quickly back to Culpeper Courthouse, which he reached on December 30, having lost on the raid, one killed, thirteen wounded, and fourteen missing. About twenty wagons and some stores had been captured. This was the fourth raid Stuart had made around or to the rear of the Federals, without capture or serious loss.

The Rev. Dr. Dabney in his *Life of Stonewall Jackson* tells us during this winter, General Jackson had for his headquarters a hunting lodge near Moss Neck. Here he was often visited by General Stuart on his rounds of official duty. These visits were always welcome to Jackson who admired and loved the young cavalry leader and they were the signal of fun for the young men of the staff. While Stuart poured out "quips and cranks" often at Jackson's expense, the latter sat by, silent and blushing, but enjoying the jests with a quiet laugh.

Confederates destroying railroad.

The walls of the lodge were ornamented with pictures which gave Stuart many a topic for jokes. Pretending to believe they had been selected by Jackson himself, he would point now to the portrait of a famous race horse and now to the print of a dog noted for his hunting feats, and remark they showed queer taste for a devout Presbyterian. Once Jackson, with a smile, replied that perhaps in his youth he had been fonder of race horses than his friends suspected.

One day, in the midst of a gay conversation, dinner was announced and the two generals with their aides passed to the mess table. The center of the table was graced by a print of butter upon which was impressed the image of a rooster. It had been presented to Jackson by a lady of the neighborhood and had been placed upon the table in honor of Stuart.

As the eyes of the gay young general fell upon it, they sparkled with glee and he exclaimed, "See there, gentlemen! We have the crowning evidence of our host's sporting tastes. He even puts his favorite gamecock upon his butter!"

The dinner, of course, began with merry laughter in which General Jackson joined with much zest.

In patriotism, in bravery, and in military skill, says Dr. Dabney, these two men were kindred spirits, but Stuart's cheerfulness and humor were the opposites of Jackson's serious and diffident temper.

Federals repairing railroad.

Though bitter cold weather had now set in, General Burnside resolved to make an effort to turn the right of General Lee's army and drive him from his winter quarters at Fredericksburg. This attempt, however, was unsuccessful, and General Burnside's failure at Fredericksburg caused him to be replaced by General Joseph Hooker, called "Fighting Joe Hooker."

Hooker reorganized the army into corps; and made one corps of the cavalry, with tried and skillful officers. He also provided the cavalry with the best horses and equipments money could procure. He realized the Federal cavalry had never been fit to contend successfully with Stuart and the forces under his command, and so now did all in his power to strengthen this branch of the Federal service. By the early spring, Hooker had his army completely reorganized and ready to begin a campaign against General Lee.

CHAPTER IX
CHANCELLORSVILLE
1863

In the meanwhile, General Lee's soldiers across the Rappahannock river suffered greatly for want of proper food and clothing during the long cold winter. The appeals of their beloved commander to the Confederate government were not heeded; but the soldiers endured their privations with great fortitude and when spring arrived, they were ready for the coming great battle with the army of "Fighting Joe Hooker."

On March 17, St. Patrick's Day, there was a cavalry engagement at Kelly's Ford, near Culpeper, where General Fitz Lee won a remarkable victory over a large force of Federal cavalry under Brigadier General Averell. Lee, who was stationed at Culpeper, had only about 800 men to meet more than 2,000 Federals, but he disposed his forces with such skill and fought so stubbornly that Averell, in spite of the fact he had a large force in reserve, was unable to break Lee's thin lines and retreated across the river.

General Stuart happened to be at Culpeper, attending a court martial, when this engagement occurred. He saw how skillfully Lee was handling the situation and unselfishly refused to assume command, wishing his able brigadier general to win all the glory of repulsing such a large force.

In this battle, John Pelham, Stuart's young chief of artillery of whom we have so often spoken, was killed. He had accompanied Stuart to Culpeper, merely on a visit of pleasure, but when he heard the call of Confederate artillery, even though it was not his own guns, he immediately went forward to take part in the engagement. Borrowing a horse from Bob Sweeny, he hurried to the battle ground. He rushed into the thickest of the fray, to rally a regiment that was beginning to waver.

Just as he shouted, "Forward, boys! forward to victory and glory!" he was mortally wounded by a fragment of a shell.

The whole South mourned the death of this young hero. James R. Randall, the author of *Maryland, My Maryland*, said of him:

"Gentlest and bravest in the battle brunt,
The Champion of the Truth,
He bore the banner to the very front Of our immortal youth."

His body was carried to Richmond and lay in state in the Capitol, until it could be borne under proper military escort to his native state, Alabama. Stuart, who loved Pelham like a son, went to Richmond to be present at the funeral.

When he wrote Mrs. Stuart of the young hero's death, he said, "His record is complete and it is spotless and noble. His character pure and his disposition as sweet and innocent as our child." The general had a strong personal affection for the young men of his staff and the death of Pelham was as great a grief to Stuart as it was a loss to the army.

Stuart's men and horses were greatly weakened by the heavy and almost constant skirmishes, picket duty, and raids in which they had been engaged since the fall. On the other hand, the Federal cavalry, just reorganized into one splendid corps under the command of Major-General George Stoneman, was in better condition than ever before. General Hooker depended upon this large and finely-equipped force to open a campaign which would prove fatal to General Lee's army.

General Stoneman was ordered to cross the Rappahannock river at one of the fords in Culpeper county and, after dispersing the small force of Confederate cavalry in that vicinity, to proceed toward Richmond, destroying the Central Railroad, capturing all supply stations, and doing all possible damage along the Pamunkey River. He was then to proceed to the Richmond and Fredericksburg Railroad, and by breaking up that road and burning certain bridges, to cut General Lee's army off from Richmond. As soon as Stoneman started on his raid, the "Grand Army," as it was called, under General Hooker himself, was to move to Chancellorsville about ten miles southwest of Fredericksburg. Thus General Lee was to be forced to come out of his entrenched position and to give battle on ground of Hooker's own choosing.

Several bodies of Federal cavalry tried to cross at various fords on the Rappahannock and Rapidan rivers, but were repulsed by small bodies of watchful Confederate pickets. The rivers were now rising rapidly from the usual spring rains, and the Rappahannock became so swollen the advance of Stoneman was checked for two weeks. Many of Stuart's troopers were absent for various reasons and he had only about two thousand men with whom to guard the fords and to cover a front of more than fifty miles.

A Pontoon Bridge made by laying timbers on wooden or canvas boats.

On the afternoon of April 24, three corps of Federal infantry appeared at Kelly's Ford. A strong party crossed in boats and drove the pickets from the ford. They then laid a pontoon bridge; and during the night, the Twelfth Army Corps passed to the southern shore. The next morning, Stuart learned the entire Grand Army was on the move. He telegraphed this information to General Lee who ordered Stuart at once to swing around the Federal divisions which had crossed the river and join him at Fredericksburg. General W. H. F. Lee with only two regiments — a small force but all that could be spared — was sent to protect the Central Railroad from Stoneman's cavalry.

Stuart, skirmishing day and night with the Federal cavalry, marched rapidly to the help of Lee. As the cavalry passed at night through the dark forest lighted only by the faint rays of a crescent moon, they had frequent alarms and several encounters with small forces of the Federal cavalry already posted in the woods.

At one time, Stuart, accompanied by only a few officers of his staff, was riding some distance ahead of his brigade, and met such a large Federal force that he was compelled to take flight. Later, when riding at the head of a regiment he had called up as an advance guard, he suddenly encountered several regiments of hostile cavalry drawn up across a field in line of battle. Stuart's small force became panic-stricken. All efforts of the general to rally his men were in vain and he was compelled a second time to retreat hastily. It seemed for a time he would be cut off from his forces, but Colonel Munford came up with his regiment, charged gallantly, captured most of the attacking Federals, and left the road again open.

Life of General J. E. B. Stuart

Several such skirmishes occurred and the troops were rendered almost panic-stricken by these unlooked-for attacks. In the darkness, they often fired on each other instead of on their foe, and they feared an ambush at each turn of the road. Altogether, it was a march of doubt and danger, but they finally reached Lee's army without serious loss.

Chancellorsville, to which place the main army of General Hooker was being moved, was not a town, but merely a large farmhouse surrounded by the usual outbuildings. Toward Fredericksburg ten miles distant, the country was somewhat open; but in every other direction it was covered with tall pines and with dense thickets of scrub oaks and many other kinds of trees and flowering plants. This forest, called "the Wilderness," was about twenty miles long and fifteen broad. It was traversed by two good roads, the Plank road and the old Turnpike; it was along these roads, the possession of which would, of course, be hotly contested by the Federal troops, that General Lee would have to send his forces to attack General Hooker in his strong position at Chancellorsville.

But on the night of the first of May, just after the first skirmishing had occurred along these two roads, Stuart brought information which changed the situation decidedly. He rode up about eleven o'clock to an old fallen tree where Lee and Jackson were talking over the plans for the next day, and reported while Hooker had fortified his position at Chancellorsville on the east, the south, and the southwest, upon the north and the west he had no defenses. At the same time, information had been secured concerning an old road by which a circuit could be made around Hooker's army. Jackson at once conceived the idea of making a forced march by this road so as to attack Hooker in the rear on the next day. Lee agreed, as on this plan seemed to depend their one chance of success.

The next morning, General Lee with about 14,000 men remained in front of the Federals on the Plank and Turnpike roads, while Jackson with three divisions marched fifteen miles through the forest and about three o'clock in the afternoon reached the rear of Hooker's army on the west. General Fitz Lee with the First Virginia cavalry led the advance while the other regiments of cavalry protected the right of Jackson's line of march. Colonel Munford, commander of one of these regiments, was familiar with this part of the country and rendered valuable service as a guide to Jackson.

As Jackson's command marched first directly south by the Furnace road, Federal scouts, who were spying from the tops of tall pine trees, thought Lee's army was in full retreat. They carried this report to Hooker who sent forward two divisions to attack the marching column. By that time, Jackson had turned to the west and, completely screened by trees and undergrowth, was marching rapidly along the old road. The rear of his column, however, was attacked near Catherine Furnace. This attack was soon checked by McLaws, whom Lee sent forward from his small force, and by two regiments sent back by Jackson when he heard the firing in his rear.

While the infantry was swinging along the forest road, the cavalry had reached the Plank road, near Chancellorsville, and was awaiting General Jackson. Fitz Lee, impatient at the delay, rode toward the Federal line, and found to his surprise it was near at hand and in full view from his post of observation. The Federals did not dream the Confederates could reach the road at this point and so had no guards stationed there.

Afterwards Fitz Lee thus described the scene: "Below and but a few hundred yards distant, ran the Federal line of battle. There was the line of defense and long lines of stacked arms in the rear. Two cannons were visible in the part of the line seen. The soldiers were in groups in the rear, laughing, chatting, smoking; probably engaged, here and there, in a game of cards and other amusements indulged in when feeling safe and awaiting orders. In the rear were other persons driving up and butchering beeves."

Realizing the importance of his discovery, Lee rode back to meet Jackson and guided him to the same place of observation. Jackson immediately placed his troops in position on the turnpike and ordered them to advance and attack the unsuspecting enemy. As long as the dense growth and rough ground permitted, Stuart and his cavalry guarded the left flank. After a rapid march through the tangled thickets, the men rushed forward with wild cheers and dashed upon the unsuspecting Federals as they were cooking their suppers. The panic-stricken Federal soldiers rushed back upon their center, and as the terror spread, after them went horses, wagons, cannon, men — speeding to recross the Rappahannock. The officers tried in vain to stop the fleeing men. For a while, the panic was so great the destruction of Hooker's army seemed certain.

After pursuing the Federals for two hours until they were within half a mile of Hooker's headquarters at the Chancellor house, the Confederates stopped in the darkness to reform. Just at this critical moment, General Hooker succeeded in bringing up reinforcements and posted fresh artillery in the edge of the woods on Hazel Grove, a small hill in front of General Jackson's assaulting column. Still, however, the soldiers in gray advanced. General A. P. Hill's division was now ordered to the front to take charge of the pursuit. While he was engaged in forming his lines, General Jackson with several aides and couriers rode down the Plank road nearly to the defenses around Chancellorsville. As they were returning, they were fired upon by some of their own men who had been posted in the thickets and who, in the moonlight, mistook Jackson and his escort for Federal cavalry.

General Jackson was wounded and was borne from the field. A little later, General Hill also was wounded. Jackson then sent for Stuart who had been ordered to hold the road to Ely's Ford, one of the Federal lines of retreat.

As soon as Stuart received the sad news that Jackson had been wounded, he placed Fitz Lee in command of the force holding the road and hastened into the heart of the Wilderness. It was midnight when he arrived at the front and according to Jackson's orders assumed command of the victorious but wearied corps. Stuart, not knowing Jackson's plans for completing the movement, sent an aide to Jackson to request instructions.

General Jackson replied, "Tell General Stuart to act upon his own judgment and do what he thinks best. I have implicit trust in him."

Such a message from his loved chieftain must have meant much to the young general who found himself suddenly confronted with such a serious situation, and the next day he proved Jackson had not trusted him in vain.

First of all, it was necessary that Stuart, who had been absent from the front sometime, should have a clear idea of the position of his men and of the Federals. He, therefore, at once called a meeting of the infantry commanders. As a result of this consultation, it was decided to defer until the next morning the attack upon the strong fortifications around Chancellorsville. The rest of the night was spent by the officers in preparations for the coming assault; the men lay upon their arms and took a brief rest.

When morning dawned, the guns of Lee, who was working his way along the two main roads to join Jackson, thundered on the east and the south, and those of Stuart answered on the west. In both wings of Lee's army, the battle raged furiously. After many assaults, Hazel Grove where

General Stonewall Jackson

the Federal artillery and infantry were posted in force, was taken by Stuart. Then arose a mighty struggle for the clearing around the Chancellor house. Stuart ordered thirty pieces of artillery to be posted so as to sweep the clearing with canister and grapeshot. Under this fire, his own men advanced, Stuart himself leading two of the charges. One of his officers said that he "looked like a very god of battle." As he rode forward at the head of his forces, he sang at the top of his clear voice which could be heard above the din of battle,

"Old Joe Hooker, Won't you come out of the wilderness?"

At the third assault, the works were carried and connection was made with General Lee's force. By ten o'clock, the Chancellor house and the woods around it, full of wounded men, were on fire from the bursting shells. The Confederate flag floated proudly in the clearing around the house and the Confederate army was again united, while Hooker's forces in full retreat were swept back into the woods north of Chancellorsville.

A great Southern historian and military critic. General Alexander, says "the promptness and boldness with which Stuart assumed command, and led the ranks of Jackson, thinned by their hard day's march and fighting to not more than 20,000 men, against Hooker's 80,000 soldiers was one of the most brilliant deeds of the war." While the battle of Chancellorsville was in progress, Stoneman, the Federal cavalry leader, had crossed the Rappahannock and was marching toward Richmond. General W. H. F. Lee followed him with two regiments and so hindered his line of march that the Federal general, in spite of his excellent cavalry, was forced to retire with few spoils and little glory. Stoneman was soon after relieved of his command, and Pleasanton was put in his place as major general of the Federal cavalry.

CHAPTER X
THE BATTLE OF BRANDY STATION
1863

Soon after the battle of Chancelorsville, Lee's army was reinforced by the return of Longstreet's corps, which had been for some time at Suffolk, Virginia, and the cavalry was increased by the addition of new regiments from North Carolina and the Shenandoah Valley. Lee's total forces were now about 80,000 and his men, encouraged by their recent victory, were in good fighting trim. Lee decided to carry the scene of war once more into northern territory. He hoped to form a line of battle near the Susquehanna river in the fertile fields of Pennsylvania, where he could force the Federals to fight on ground of his own choosing. The next weeks were spent in preparation for this northward movement.

On June 6, there was a cavalry review on the open plain between Culpeper Courthouse and Brandy Station. Great preparations had been made for this review. Each trooper had burnished his weapons and trappings and rubbed down his much-enduring charger in order that they might make the best appearance possible. Visitors, especially many ladies, from all the country round attended the magnificent spectacle.

Stuart and his entire staff took their position on a little grassy knoll. Eight thousand troopers and sixteen pieces of horse artillery passed before him in columns of squadrons — first at a walk, then at a gallop — while the guns of a battery on a hill opposite the reviewing stand fired at regular intervals.

An eyewitness of the scene tells us that Stuart was superbly mounted. The trappings on his proud, prancing horse all looked bright and new and his sidearms gleamed in the morning sun like burnished silver. A long black ostrich plume waved gracefully from a drab slouch hat cocked up on one side and held by a clasp which also stayed the plume."

The same authority, Gunner Neese, tells an amusing story about himself during this review. He says that, as acting first sergeant of his battery, he was riding at the head of the horse artillery, mounted on a mule with ears about a foot long. Just before the artillery arrived at the reviewing stand, the searching eye of General Stuart, who was very fastidious in all things, spied the waving ears of the mule and he quickly dispatched an aide to tell the captain to order the mule and his rider off the field. Neese says he was not greatly surprised at the order, but that the mule was.

For sometime General Hooker had wanted to know what was going on behind the dense screen of cavalry Stuart had collected at Culpeper, for it was evident General Lee was planning an important movement. Just two days after the big review, Hooker sent to find out, and for once the Federal cavalry took Stuart by surprise. General Pleasanton marched cautiously to the north bank of the Rappahannock, at Beverly's Ford, with three divisions of cavalry and five brigades of infantry. No fires were allowed in the Federal camp, and every precaution was taken to prevent the Confederate pickets on the south bank from discovering the presence of the large force.

Stuart's brigades, under Fitz Lee, Robertson, W. H. F. Lee, and Jones, were encamped near the fords of the Rappahannock in readiness to cross the river the next morning and protect the flank of Lee's army which was already beginning its northward movement. Four batteries of horse artillery were encamped in the edge of the woods, in advance of Jones's brigade, near St. James Church. This church was about two hundred yards to the west of the direct road to Beverly^s Ford and was about two miles from the ford.

Stuart himself camped on Fleetwood Hill, half a mile east of Brandy Station and four miles from Beverly's Ford. As an early start was ordered for the next morning, all of Stuart's camp equipage was packed in wagons in readiness for the move. Pickets were placed at all fords and the weary men slept, unaware of the lurking enemy.

At dawn on June 9, General Pleasanton divided his command into two columns and sent one, under Brigadier General Gregg, to cross the river at Kelly's Ford, four miles below the railroad bridge, and to gain the road to Culpeper Courthouse. The other column, under General Buford, was ordered to cross at Beverly's Ford and proceed toward Brandy Station. This advance was gallantly disputed by the Confederate pickets at the ford, but being greatly outnumbered they were retiring slowly toward St. James Church when Major Flournoy with about one hundred men charged down the road upon the advancing regiments. The colonel who was leading the Federal charge was killed and the troops were driven back.

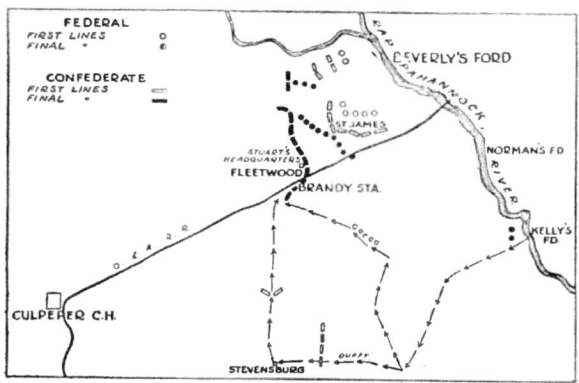

Map of the Battle of Brandy Station.

But the skirmishes of the picket force and the charge of Major Flournoy had given General Jones time to draw up his men in line of battle and to withdraw the artillery from its exposed position. General Jones then charged to the support of Major Flournoy. This charge was repelled by the Federals, and Jones retired to his line of battle at St. James Church where he was soon joined by the brigades of Hampton and W. H. F. Lee.

From ten o'clock in the morning, the battle raged furiously. The Confederates advanced, but were met by Federal troops that charged gallantly across an open field up to the very muzzles of the cannon which were sending forth shell and canister into their midst. They advanced, however, too far beyond their guns and, being attacked on both flanks, they retreated with heavy loss.

Stuart, who had hastened to the front to dispute the march of Buford, was suddenly threatened by more serious danger in the rear.

The gallant Colonel Butler had been left with a regiment of South Carolina cavalry to guard Brandy Station, two miles in the rear of St. James Church and just half a mile from Fleetwood Hill where Stuart's headquarters had been located for several weeks. While on duty at Brandy Station, Colonel Butler was informed by a scout that a body of Federal cavalry was moving toward Stevensburg. This was a part of the column which had been sent to Kelly's Ford early in the morning. General Gregg had driven in the Confederate pickets at the ford, and although General Robertson moved at once to the help of his pickets, he was too late to prevent General Gregg from sending a considerable force toward Stevensburg which was on the direct road to Culpeper Courthouse where General Lee was encamped. General Gregg himself, with the remainder of his force, marched on toward Brandy Station.

Colonel Butler knew it was most important to keep the Federals from finding out Lee's army was at Culpeper, and as soon as he heard they were marching along the Stevensburg road, he advanced without orders down that road. After a fierce fight, he stopped the advance of the Federals who turned back to join Gregg at Brandy Station.

In the meantime, General Gregg had marched to the station where, Colonel Butler being absent, he met no opposing force. From this point, he immediately passed on to Fleetwood Hill which that morning had been vacated by General Stuart as headquarters. Stuart had left there Major H. B. McClellan and several couriers, with orders for all brigades and regiments to communicate with him at that place. These staff officers saw Gregg's large forces approaching and knew that they must hold the hill at any cost, as it was the key to Stuart's whole position.

In Major McClellan's *Life of Stuart* he gives us a very vivid and accurate account of the combats which raged up and down and over the crest of Fleetwood Hill. He says every vestige of the camp had been removed and there remained upon the hill only McClellan and the couriers. A six-pound howitzer, which for want of ammunition had been sent back from the fight going on at St. James Church, was halted at the foot of the hill and later proved their salvation. As soon as the young major saw the long Federal columns approaching, he dispatched a courier to General Stuart with information of this movement. For fear some accident might befall the first courier, he sent a second, praying for help lest the entire force be enclosed between the divisions of Buford and Gregg.

Finding some round shot and imperfect shells in the limber chest. Major McClellan ordered the howitzer to be brought up the hill and a slow fire to be opened upon the rapidly-advancing Federals. The fire caused surprise and a halt. It seemed to indicate the presence of a considerable force.

General Gregg, therefore, made preparations for a serious attack upon the hill, and opened fire with three rifled guns. But Major McClellan and the men with their one gun, held the hill until help came. Reinforcements promptly sent by General Stuart arrived just as the lieutenant in charge of the gun had fired his last cartridge and the Federal cavalry was advancing "in magnificent order of columns of squadrons, with flags and guidons flying."

There now followed a number of combats which for dash and bravery have rarely been equaled. First the Confederates, then the Federals, seemed to have possession of the hill. Stuart himself soon arrived, bringing Hampton and Jones from the other firing line to help hold this important position. Back and forth swept the blue and the gray, each fighting stubbornly and well. For a brief space of time, the New Jersey cavalry held the hill. Soon they were repulsed by a charge led by the Virginia cavalry. There was a fierce contest at the foot of the hill over three Federal guns. The Confederates charged and took the guns, but were driven back by overwhelming numbers and forced to cut their way out. About this time, Hampton came up with his four regiments formed in columns of squadrons with a battery of four guns. As they advanced at a gallop, they saw the crest of Fleetwood Hill covered with Federal cavalry. Passing the eastern side of the hill, they struck the column just beyond the railroad and there followed a fierce hand-to-hand fight. When the smoke and dust of the conflict lifted, it was seen Hampton had won. The Federals were retiring. At the same time, a charge had been made straight up the hill on the northeast side by Georgia and South Carolina cavalry. A saber charge was made and the hill was cleared of the opposing troops. As soon as the Confederates gained the summit of the hill, three batteries were placed in position there.

Fleetwood Hill was now in the possession of the Confederates, but the Federals still held Brandy Station. Stuart at once brought up a regiment which charged on both sides of the road to the station, drove out the Federals and pursued them for some distance.

While the battle was raging at Fleetwood Hill, W. H. F. Lee with a small force held the Confederate lines near St. James Church. There was a lull in the fighting while Buford was retiring some of his cavalry and bringing up fresh troops, and so Stuart was able to withdraw both Hampton and Jones, in order to repel the attack on Fleetwood Hill.

As soon as the Federals were driven from Brandy Station, Stuart formed a new line of battle between the church and the station, where he received a heavy Federal onset. This battle was waged with varied success, but at last Gregg joined Buford and late in the evening the Federals retired across the river — defeated in spite of their superior numbers.

The losses in the battle of Brandy Station were heavy on both sides. The Federal loss was nearly 1,000 officers and men, while the Confederate loss was more than 500. The Federals were forced to leave in the hands of the Confederates three cannon, six flags, and nearly 500 prisoners. Pleasanton was really driven back by Stuart and the cavalry, but he claimed that as he had found out that there was a force of infantry at Culpeper Courthouse, which was the information he had been sent to obtain, he retired as soon as possible after he had been joined by Gregg.

Gunner Neese tells us several times during the day he saw General Stuart, when the battle raged fiercest, dash with his staff across the field and pass from point to point along the line, perfectly heedless of the surrounding danger. During the engagement, Neese fired his faithful gun one hundred and sixty times. Just before the battle closed in the evening he saw the fire flash from the cascabel of his gun and found that it was disabled forever — burnt out entirely at the breech.

We have described this battle at length because it is considered one of the greatest cavalry combats of the nineteenth century.

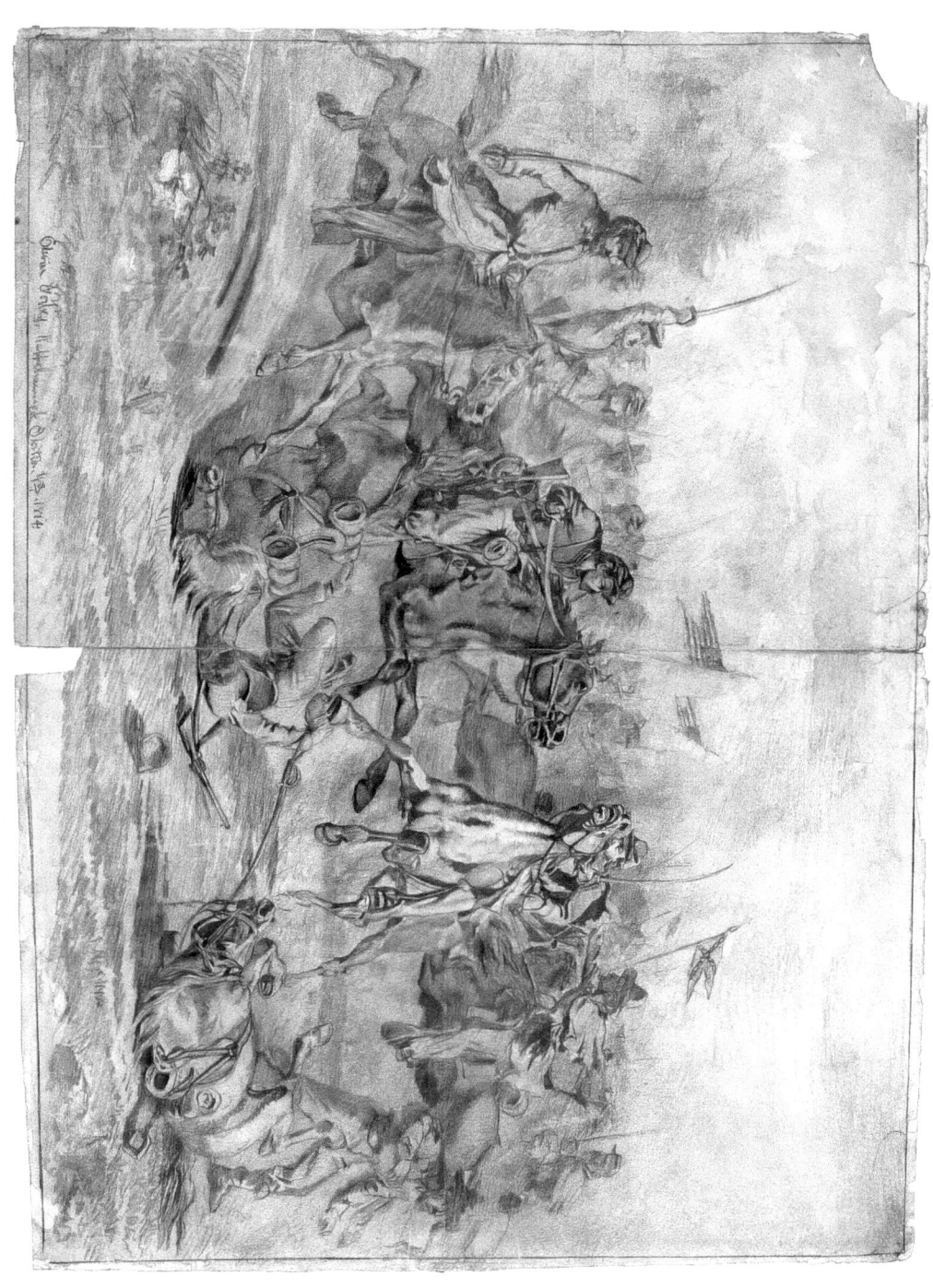

Battle of Brandy Station.

CHAPTER XI
THE GETTYSBURG CAMPAIGN
1863

Stuart did not attempt to follow Pleasanton, because Lee's plan for the invasion of the North would not allow the useless sacrifice of men and horses. Indeed, all of the cavalry was needed to screen his army as it marched through the Blue Ridge gaps into the Valley, from which point it was to cross the Potomac into Maryland.

While Longstreet's Corps, which was the last to move from Culpeper, was advancing to the Valley, Stuart and his cavalry had a hard time trying to protect Ashby's and Snicker's gaps, through which Longstreet's forces would have to pass. The battles of Aldie, Middleburg, and Upperville, severe cavalry engagements in which Stuart's forces were slowly forced back to the foot of the Blue Ridge, were all fought to protect these gaps until Longstreet could pass through them on his northward march.

On June 22, General Pleasanton, who had forced General Stuart back from Upperville to Ashby's Gap, withdrew, and Stuart moved forward to Rector's Cross Roads, where he could better watch the Federal movements. On that same day, General Ewell, who commanded the advance division of General Lee's army, crossed the Potomac. By June 27, Lee's entire army had reached Chambersburg, Pennsylvania.

In the meantime, Stuart was in Virginia watching the Federals, in order to report to Lee the moment Hooker began to move. He wrote General Lee that he thought he could move with some of his cavalry around General Hooker's rear into Maryland, thus throwing himself between the Federals and Washington, and so probably delay Hooker's northward movement. General Lee wanted General Stuart and his cavalry to join General Early and guard his flank as he marched toward York, Pennsylvania; he thought Stuart could reach him in this way just as easily as by crossing at Shepherdstown where the rest of the army crossed. Therefore, he gave Stuart permission to cross at one of the lower fords, telling him to annoy the Federals in the rear and collect all possible supplies for the army.

Major Von Borcke, the young Prussian officer, had been severely wounded and Major McClellan was now Stuart's adjutant general. He tells us on the night before General Stuart started, a cold drizzling rain was falling, but the general insisted on sleeping on the ground under a tree, because he said his men were exposed to the rain and he would not fare better than they. He could have had more comfortable quarters on the porch of a deserted house near by, where McClellan, by the light of a tallow "dip," was receiving and writing dispatches. When General Lee's letter, containing instructions for Stuart's march, came, McClellan carried it to the general, who quietly read it, and then turned to go to sleep on his hard, cold bed.

It was by such an example as this, as well as by his bravery in battle, that Stuart won the undying love of his soldiers. I am going to quote for you a beautiful tribute paid him by Mosby, his chief scout, who guided Stuart past the Federal lines on the first part of this expedition.

Mosby says when he went to the general for instructions before starting, "he was in his usual gay humor. I never saw him at any time in any other. Always buoyant in spirits, he inspired with his own high hopes all who came in contact with him. I felt the deepest affection for him. My chief ambition was to serve him. He was the rare combination of the Puritan and the knight-errant — he felt intensely the joy of battle and he loved the praise of fair women and brave men.

"I served under him from the beginning of the war until he closed his life, like Sidney, leading a squadron on the field of honor. Yet I do not remember that he ever gave me an order. There was always so much sympathy between us and I felt so much affection for him that he had only to express a wish, that was an order for me."

In making their plans, neither Lee nor Stuart had counted on an immediate northward movement of the Federal army. Yet when Stuart with three brigades passed eastward through a gap in Bull Run Mountain, he found Hooker's army already moving northward. He at once sent General Lee a dispatch conveying this valuable information, but the courier bearing it never reached headquarters, and so Lee did not know of this important movement until Hooker's whole army had crossed the Potomac and moved toward Frederick, Maryland.

It was now impossible for Stuart to cross the river where he had intended, and it would take too much time to retrace his steps and cross at Shepherdstown, so he determined on the bold move of crossing at Rowser's Ford, or Seneca, only thirteen miles from Washington city. At this point, the water was very deep and swift, and the artillery had difficulty in crossing, but time was too precious for them to seek a better ford.

The caissons and limber chests were emptied and dragged through the water, and the ammunition was carried over in the hands of troopers. By three o'clock on the morning of June 28, Stuart's command was on the Maryland side of the river, but the whole Federal army now lay between the cavalry and General Lee. Stuart would have to march around this army before he could obey Lee's order to join Early at York.

But General Lee had also told Stuart to collect all the supplies he could get for the use of the army. He now had an opportunity to carry out these instructions, for he met and captured a long line of Federal supply wagons.

Fitz Lee's brigade tore up the track of the Baltimore and Ohio Railroad, burned the bridge, and cut the telegraph wires, thus destroying the line of communication between Washington City and General Meade who had taken Hooker's place as commander of the Federal forces. At one time, Stuart's troopers were so near Washington they could see the dome of the Capitol, and the whole North was in a panic lest the dreaded Stuart should attack the city. General Stuart, however, was hastening northward in order to join General Early at York.

His long train of captured wagons seriously hindered the rapid movement of his horsemen, but he was unwilling to abandon these supplies he knew were so greatly needed by Lee's army.

If, however, he could have foreseen the events of the next few days he would have burned the wagons and hurried by forced marches to join General Lee who had to fight the first two days' battle at Gettysburg without the valuable aid of Stuart and his cavalry. But Stuart acted in the light of what he knew and did what seemed best at the time, holding on to his valuable prize in spite of the fact it delayed his march to York nearly two days.

On the morning of June 30, Stuart had a sharp encounter with cavalry, at Hanover, Pennsylvania, and at one time it seemed he would have to give up his captured wagons. He already had them parked, so they could easily be burned if he was compelled to leave them, but Hampton's and Fitz Lee's brigades, which had been guarding the wagons in the rear, came up and the Federals were dislodged.

Stuart remained at Hanover until night, in order to hold the Federals in check, while the wagon trains were sent toward York under the protection of Fitz Lee's brigade.

Major McClellan tells us this night's march was terrible to both the troopers and the drivers of the wagons. The men were hungry and exhausted, and so were the mules. Every time a wagon stopped, it caused a halt along the whole line, and as the drivers were constantly falling asleep, these halts occurred very frequently. It required the utmost vigilance on the part of every officer on Stuart's staff to keep the train in motion.

When Fitz Lee reached the road leading from York to Gettysburg, he learned Early had already marched westward. When Stuart arrived at this point, he sent out couriers to find Early and locate the other Confederate forces. He then pushed immediately on to Carlisle where he hoped to obtain provisions for his weary and hungry troops, but when he reached Carlisle, he found it already in possession of the Federals.

Smith, the Federal general in command, was summoned to surrender, but he replied, "If you want the city, come and take it."

Stuart was preparing to storm the city when he received orders from General Lee to move at once toward Gettysburg.

For eight days and nights, Stuart's men had been almost continually on the march and had been surrounded by superior cavalry forces, but "he reached Gettysburg on the evening of the second of July, in time to take part in the third day's battle. He delivered to the quartermaster one hundred and twenty-five captured wagons and teams. He would willingly have sacrificed this valuable prize could he have been on hand two days earlier to assist his beloved chief in the battle that had been unexpectedly forced at this point, but in which he held his ground during two days of stubborn fighting.

General Lee's plan for the third day's battle was to have General Longstreet's Corps storm the Federal center in its strongly-fortified position upon Cemetery Ridge. Stuart's cavalry was to march unobserved to the Federal rear. Here it was to attack, thus protecting the Confederate left flank and drawing attention away from the forces which were to storm Cemetery Ridge.

About noon on the third of July, Stuart led two brigades along the York turnpike and took position on Cross Ridge in the rear of the Federal line of battle. Hampton and Fitz Lee were ordered to follow as soon as they were supplied with ammunition.

On the slope of Cross Ridge stood a stone dairy, and farther down in the valley was a barn belonging to a farmer named Rummel. Concealing his men in the woods on the top of the hill, Stuart pushed forward a gun and fired a number of shots, probably to notify General Lee he had gained a good position on the left flank. He then sent word for Hampton and Fitz Lee to hasten, as he wished to attack the Federal rear. While waiting for them, he sent some dismounted cavalry to hold the Rummel barn and a fence to the right of it.

Before Fitz Lee and Hampton came up, Stuart saw he had stirred up a hornet's nest.

The Federal cavalry had discovered his movements and were ready for him. A battery of six guns opened fire upon his gun and soon disabled it. Then a strong line of sharpshooters advanced and a fierce fight took place near the barn. On the left, the Confederate sharpshooters drove the Federals for some distance across the field. Just then a large force of Federal cavalry appeared and drove back the Confederate dismounted men almost to the Rummel barn. There the Federals were met and driven back by the Confederates, but the Federals were reinforced and returned. Hampton advanced to the charge, and the battle surged back and forth over the open field in a hand-to-hand fight with pistols and sabers, until nearly all of Hampton's and Fitz Lee's regiments were engaged.

At last the Federals retired to the line held at the beginning of the fight and the Confederates held the Rummel barn. There followed an artillery duel which lasted until night. Then Stuart withdrew to the York turnpike, leaving a regiment of cavalry picketed around the barn which was full of wounded Confederates.

Stuart encamped that night on the York road. Early the next morning, he withdrew in the rain and rejoined the main army on the heights west of Gettysburg. The Confederates under Pickett had stormed the Federal heights opposite and had taken the guns, but as Hood, who was to support the charge was detained by the Federal cavalry, they could not hold their position, and finally had to retreat with the loss of many lives. The Federals did not pursue the Confederates, but remained the whole of the next day upon their entrenched heights.

Being now nearly out of ammunition and supplies for his men. General Lee ordered a retreat on the night of July 4. He had a difficult task to perform. But happily his army had not been routed nor had the men lost confidence in him. As long as he was leading, they were willing to go anywhere and to endure anything.

He had now before him a long march, and he was encumbered with four thousand prisoners and a wagon train fifteen miles long. It would take great skill and courage to conduct his army safely back into Virginia.

In this extremity, he relied on his cavalry for aid. Both men and horses were by this time reduced in numbers and were worn out by hunger and fatigue. They, however, took promptly the position assigned by General Lee and guarded the army and its trains from the attacks of the Federal cavalry. General Stuart's command guarded both wings of the army — Stuart himself being on one side and Fitz Lee on the other. They, of course, were pursued by the Federal cavalry, and before they reached the fords of the Potomac, both Stuart and Fitz Lee had been engaged in several skirmishes.

The wagon train reached Williamsport on July 6, and found the river too much swollen to cross. The wagons were massed in a narrow space near the river and were guarded by a small force. Here they were attacked by General Buford. This engagement is called "the Teamsters' Battle," because the teamsters assisted the troopers so well in holding the Federals in check. Together they succeeded in resisting the attack of Buford until the arrival of Stuart who had been engaged in driving the Federal cavalry from Hagerstown. A little later, Fitz Lee came thundering down the Greencastle road. Buford then retired without having taken or destroyed the trains so important to Lee.

On July 7, when the infantry and artillery arrived at Hagerstown from which Stuart had driven the Federal cavalry the day before. General Lee was not able to cross the Potomac. He, therefore, selected a strong position and fortified it while waiting for the waters to fall. From July 8 to 12, Stuart protected the front of Lee's army, fighting a number of battles. Then, all the Federal forces having come up, Stuart retired to the main body of the army and General Lee prepared for battle. But Meade, who was very cautious, thought Lee's position too strong to attack.

Major McClellan, General Stuart's adjutant general, says in his *Life of Stuart* those days will be remembered by the cavalry leader's staff as days of great hardship. The country had been swept bare of provisions and nothing could be purchased. Scanty rations had been issued to the men, but none to the officers. For four or five days, they received all the food they had from a young lady in Hagerstown, whose father, a Southerner, loved the Confederacy. After a day of incessant fighting, Stuart and his

A Federal wagon park.

officers reached the house of this friend about nine o'clock at night. While food was being prepared, Stuart fell asleep on the sofa in the parlor. When supper was announced, he refused to rise. Knowing he had eaten nothing for twenty-four hours. Major McClellan took him by the arm and compelled him to take his place at the table. He ate sparingly and without relish.

Thinking that the supper did not suit him their kind hostess inquired: "General, perhaps you would like to have a hard-boiled egg?" "Yes" he replied, "I'll take four or five." This singular reply caused a good deal of astonishment, but nothing was said at the time. The eggs were brought in; Stuart broke one and ate it, and rose from the table.

When they returned to the parlor, Major McClellan sat down at the piano and commenced singing,

> "If you want to have a good time
> Jine the cavalry."

The circumstances hardly made the song appropriate, but the chorus roused the general and he joined in it with a right good will. During all that time, he had been unconscious of his surroundings, and when told of his seeming rudeness to his hostess he hastened to make apologies.

This little incident shows how greatly Stuart was exhausted by the strain and fatigue of sleepless days and nights during this unfortunate campaign. For more than two weeks, he had been almost constantly in the saddle, using both mind and body in the effort to save his command and to bring the Confederate army back to Virginia without serious disaster.

On July 13, the waters had subsided so much General Lee gave orders for the army to cross the river that night. By one o'clock the next afternoon, the Southern army was again in Virginia, General Stuart's command bringing up the rear.

The Federals, strange to say, offered little opposition and the crossing was a complete success. The Federal government and the northern people were much disappointed when they learned General Lee had so skillfully led his army out of its perilous position. They had expected General Meade would destroy it, hemmed in between the flooded Potomac and the Federal army so superior in numbers. Lee now moved back to Bunker Hill near Winchester. Stuart repelled an advance of the Federal cavalry and drove it steadily back to within a mile of Shepherdstown. Here a large number of the troopers were dismounted and advanced in line of battle. The Federals retreated slowly until dark when they withdrew from the contest in the direction of Harper's Ferry, having lost heavily in killed and wounded.

CHAPTER XII
FINAL CAMPAIGNS AND DEATH
1863-'64

General Meade now advanced into Virginia and attempted to follow General Lee and cut him off from Richmond. Lee being at once informed by Stuart of the movement, skillfully eluded his foe and by the first of August, had placed his army behind the Rappahannock River, between Meade and Richmond.

The cavalry now had a short period of rest. The whole force was reorganized, and Hampton and Fitz Lee were promoted to the rank of major general. This much-needed rest was broken on September 13, by the advance of the Federals into Culpeper county. Stuart had been warned of their forward movement, and at once started his wagons and disabled horses toward Rapidan Station. General Lee supposing General Meade was advancing in force, had already retired behind the Rapidan River and placed his army in a very strong position.

Early on the morning of Sept. 13, the Federal cavalry advanced in large numbers to the fords of the Rappahannock. As Lee did not intend to hold Culpeper county, Stuart retired toward Rapidan Station, keeping up a running fight as he withdrew.

A few days later, Stuart came in touch with Buford's Cavalry near Jack's Shop in Madison County, and attacked them in several spirited charges. He was unable, however, to drive back these forces. Unwilling to retreat, he advanced and was engaged in a furious combat when he was informed Kilpatrick's command was in his rear. As he withdrew to meet this unexpected foe, Buford pressed forward and it seemed for a time Stuart had at last been caught in a place from which he could not escape.

Kilpatrick had already thrown a large force of dismounted men between Stuart and the river, and he was thus enclosed between two large forces of finely-mounted men. Buford pressed forward until the battle was brought into a field in the center of which a small hill afforded a good position for Stuart's artillery. He now divided his regiments and guns — some to fight Buford, some to fight Kilpatrick. At last, Kilpatrick's main force was driven back and one of Stuart's regiments dashed up to the fence behind which Kilpatrick's dismounted men were firing, threw it down, and made way for Stuart to retire. Withdrawing rapidly, Stuart then crossed the ford at Liberty Mills where he was very soon reinforced.

The toll of war. Dead Confederates on the battlefield at Gettysburg.

On October 9, General Lee commenced the movement around the right of General Meade's army which is called the "Bristoe Campaign." In this campaign, the cavalry was sorely tried. Fitz Lee — who, as you have been told, had been promoted to the rank of major general— was left at Raccoon Ford, supported by two brigades of infantry, to hold Lee's line and to make Meade believe Lee's whole army was still encamped at that place. Stuart with Hampton's Division moved to the right of Lee's army as it again marched northward; it was his duty to prevent the Federals from finding out Lee's movements and to protect the army from attacks.

Now followed a series of sharp engagements between the cavalry of the two armies. There was a skirmish near James City after which the Federals retired toward Culpeper Courthouse. The next morning, Stuart followed them. Three miles from the Courthouse, he met and drove in the Federal pickets. But he now found out Meade was retreating from the Rappahannock and Fitz Lee, who had fought a battle at Raccoon Ford, was advancing towards Brandy Station, — fighting Buford as he marched.

Stuart knew that Kilpatrick was at Culpeper Courthouse awaiting his attack, but on receiving this news he turned at once northward toward Brandy Station, hoping to join Fitz Lee and get possession of Fleetwood Hill from which he had driven the Federal cavalry in June. If he could carry out this plan, he would cut off Kilpatrick from Buford. Kilpatrick, who had massed his force of about four thousand men on the open space east of the Courthouse at Culpeper waiting the attack of Stuart, soon found out the latter had eluded him and was hurrying toward Brandy Station. He, therefore, began a race for the same position.

Unfortunately, Stuart was delayed by a skirmish with Federal forces and when he came in sight of Brandy Station, he saw that Kilpatrick had beaten him in the race. Buford, who was being pursued by Fitz Lee, had already taken possession of Fleetwood Hill and placed his artillery upon its crest. Stuart had moved so rapidly he had left his artillery far behind, but Fitz Lee's guns were booming as he came into position.

Fitz Lee joined Stuart and they at once attacked Kilpatrick's and Buford's forces, now under the command of Major General Pleasanton. The Federals fought bravely, but they were steadily pushed toward their position on Fleetwood Hill. It was now late in the afternoon, and Stuart, declining to attack them in their strong position, sent Fitz Lee to the left as if to cut off the Federals from the river. As soon as Pleasanton perceived this flanking movement, he withdrew from Fleetwood Hill and, protected by his artillery, crossed the river. Stuart's weary troopers camped that night once more around Brandy Station, well pleased at having gained a decided victory over such large forces.

Two days later, Stuart reached Warrenton where the whole army was encamped and he immediately received orders to proceed toward Catlett's Station with two thousand men and seven guns, for the purpose of gaining accurate information about the position of Meade's army.

General Meade had started his forces back toward Culpeper Courthouse to engage General Lee in battle, but he found out Lee was marching around his right, so as to get between him and Washington City. On receiving this information, Meade at once recalled his forces.

These movements and counter movements came near resulting disastrously to Stuart who was caught between the advancing and retreating divisions of the Federals.

When he reached Catlett's Station, he found a column of Federal infantry was moving toward that place. He at once fell back on the road to Warrenton and found another Federal corps in his rear. His situation was now one of great peril. It seemed his force would either be captured or cut to pieces.

Fortunately, when Stuart perceived his danger he was emerging from a piece of woods and night was closing in. He at once retired his command to the depths of the woods and called a council of his officers. They were so near the enemy that the neighing of a horse or the clash of a saber could be heard, and to make retreat impossible, they were hemmed in on one side by a swollen stream and on the other side by a forest.

At first, it was proposed to leave the seven guns and cut their way out. Stuart, however, would not agree to abandon his artillery. At last, officers went through the command and ordered each man to stand by his horse's head, and to make no sound himself nor let his horse make any.

As soon as it was dark, Stuart ordered four trusted men to make their way to General Lee at Culpeper Courthouse. They were to inform him of the dangerous position of the cavalry and ask him to send aid as soon as possible. Then followed long hours of anxious waiting. During the night, a Federal corps marched past the front of Stuart's position, but fortunately the noise of the moving column prevented the Federals from detecting the presence of the Confederates within the woods.

At the first peep of day, the Confederates discovered a large force of Federal infantry had halted near, had stacked arms, and were getting breakfast. They were so near the Confederates that several of their officers who strayed into the woods were captured. In the dim light of morning, each soldier in gray tightened the girth of his hungry, weary steed and mounted silently, with weapons ready for the charge. The seven guns were parked near the west of the hill, just opposite the feasting Federals. Then the men waited — waited either to be discovered by the Federals when the bright sunlight should flash upon their gray coats or to hear Lee's guns as a signal for them to attack.

At last! There was firing from toward Warrenton. Aid was approaching and the time had come to cut their way out. In an instant, the seven guns were pouring shot and shell upon the surprised Federals. The horsemen then charged upon the infantry regiments which had hastily formed in line of battle and were advancing upon the guns. A fierce combat now ensued in which the Federals were driven back. The artillery and wagons, followed closely by the horsemen, passed behind the rear of the Federals and thus the whole command escaped from its perilous position.

General Meade now fell back to Centerville and General Lee, having failed to cut off General Meade from Washington, retired again to the line of the Rappahannock. Stuart continued to follow the Federal cavalry, having skirmishes at Bull Run, Groveton, and Frying Pan Church.

A few days later, the Confederate cavalry defeated a large force of infantry near Buckland, in a battle that is known as the "Buckland Races." After a sharp skirmish, Stuart fell back slowly toward Warrenton in order to draw the Federals after him; for Fitz Lee was moving forward from Warrenton to attack them in the rear. Stuart, as soon as he heard the sound of Fitz Lee's guns, turned suddenly upon the Federals with so furious a charge that their lines were broken and put to flight. Stuart chased, them for five miles and captured two hundred and fifty prisoners and eight wagons and ambulances. Thus he may be said to have fairly won the race back to Buckland.

Soon after this, both armies went into winter quarters. The Federal soldiers had comforts and even luxuries, while the Confederates were poorly clothed and fed. Their sufferings during this bitter cold winter could not have been endured but for the food and clothing sent from their homes. Officers and men fared alike; the resources of the Confederacy were at a low ebb.

Mrs. Stuart was boarding at Orange Courthouse, and, as General Stuart's headquarters were near by, he was able to spend some time with his family again. And a very happy family it was now, for on the ninth of the previous October, the very day which began Stuart's heavy work in the Bristoe Campaign, a daughter had come to comfort him and Mrs. Stuart for the loss of their little Flora. The devoted father named this little baby Virginia Pelham, in honor of his beloved state and in memory of the gallant young leader of the Stuart Horse Artillery whom he had loved so well. The members of General Stuart's staff were all devoted to this new member of the family, and General Lee, whose headquarters were not far distant, came more than once to visit Mrs. Stuart and "Miss Virginia" as he called the little lady. The admiration paid his little daughter gave Stuart great delight.

Late in February, 1864, the Federal cavalry made an attempt to take Richmond. This movement was known as "Dahlgren's Raid" and the large Federal forces were fitted out with great care. But in spite of their superior numbers, they were driven back by Stuart's cavalry.

On March 17, General U. S. Grant was placed in command of all the Federal armies. As it was evident the great struggle of the year would take place in Virginia, he took charge of General Meade's army and prepared it for the coming campaign. He had an army of 125,000 men, fully equipped, and with all that money could buy.

At midnight on May 3, the Federal army began to advance. General Lee permitted it to cross the Rapidan and march into the Wilderness where the battle of Chancellorsville had been fought the year before. In this jungle, it would be difficult for the Federals to use their artillery and they would be compelled to fight at a disadvantage: General Grant expected General Lee to retreat to a line nearer Richmond, and he was surprised when his troops plunged into the dense woods and thickets of the Wilderness to find General Lee ready to fight on ground of his own choosing.

As soon as the news was received at the cavalry headquarters that the Federals had crossed the fords of the Rapidan, Stuart set out for his picket line. He conducted in person the advances of the infantry until the lines of the enemy were reached, and on May 6 and 7 the great Battle of the Wilderness raged furiously.

The cavalry did heavy work on the Confederate right. Gunner Neese, in his diary, tells an interesting anecdote of Stuart on the morning of the second day's battle.

He says: "Our orders to hasten to the front this morning at daylight were pressing and urgent, and we had no time to prepare or eat breakfast, which greatly ruffled some of our drivers. When we drew near to the enemy's line we awaited orders, and one of our drivers was still going through baby acts about something to eat and having no breakfast. Just then General Stuart and staff came along and halted a moment right in the road where we were and heard the grumbling and childish murmuring of our hungry man, and the general rode up to him and gave him two biscuits out of his own haversack."

On the night of May 7, Grant began to move his army by the left flank to get between Lee and Richmond, but the movement was discovered at once and Fitz Lee's cavalry was sent forward to delay the Federals until Longstreet's infantry could come up. Fitz Lee's men were at times dismounted, and they fought so stubbornly that Grant's forces were held in check until the infantry by a rapid night march reached the entrenchments which had been hastily thrown up near Spotsylvania Courthouse.

I am going to tell you about the arrival of the infantry and the beginning of the next morning's battle in the words of a private of the First Virginia cavalry.

He says: "We had been fighting and retreating all night, and at last, when near Spotsylvania Courthouse had thrown up slight entrenchments. Protected by Breathed's guns, we were awaiting another attack. Suddenly we heard the steady march of infantry coming in our rear. The old fellows came swinging along in the moonlight, each one with his camp-kettle on his back and his long musket with its gleaming bayonet resting easily on his shoulder. Each man settled down by a dismounted trooper, glad to rest a little while, but full of quips and jokes. 'Look here sonny,' said one to me, picking up my carbine, 'What's this here thing for? Ef I was you I'd be feared of it; it might hurt somebody!' But even talking was not permitted. Officers passed along, enjoining silence and ordering us not to fire until we could see the whites of the Yankees' eyes.

"About daylight we heard loud cheering. Major Breathed had brought off one of his guns in the face of thousands of the enemy, and they were cheering! On came a blue line of battle eight deep calling out, 'Come out, you dismounted cavalry! We know you are there.'

"Silence reigned behind the earthworks, but every gun was ready. When the Federals were well over the crest of the hill, the order rang along the line — 'Steady, aim, fire!' Bang! went the carbines and muskets, and with piercing yells the Confederates leaped out of the works and rushed with gleaming bayonets upon the already retreating foe. The veterans had delivered so fierce and so well-directed a fire that the attack was not renewed at that position."

A short while afterward, Stuart arrived with reinforcements. Major McClellan was the only member of General Stuart's staff present during the brisk skirmishes of the morning. He says Stuart exposed himself recklessly to the fire of the Federals, in spite of the earnest request of the infantry officers that he would retire to a safer position.

He sent Major McClellan on such seemingly unnecessary messages that after a while that officer thought General Stuart was trying to shield him from danger, so he said, "General, my horse is weary. You are exposing yourself and you are alone. Please let me remain with you."

But Stuart merely smiled kindly and sent him with another message.

When Grant reached Spotsylvania Courthouse, he decided to send a corps of cavalry forward on a raid toward Richmond. This force was to cut Lee's communication, take Richmond, and be in position to attack the rear of Lee's army after Grant crushed him at Spotsylvania. General Sheridan commanded these troops that started for Richmond, along the Telegraph Road.

General Fitz Lee who saw them, says: "Ten thousand horsemen riding in a single road in column of fours made a column thirteen miles in length; and with flashing sabers and fluttering guidons were an imposing array."

To contend with this force, Stuart had only three small brigades, yet on him depended the safety of Richmond and the protection of the rear of Lee's army. At Jarrold's Mill, Wickham's brigade had a sharp skirmish with Sheridan's rear guard and captured a number of prisoners. Yet on and on marched Sheridan, leaving the Telegraph Road, and going toward Beaver Dam Station. At Mitchell's Shop, Sheridan's rear guard having been reenforced, made another stand. Wickham attacked again, but would have been forced back by the greatly-superior numbers of the Federals had not Stuart and Fitz Lee come up with reinforcements and the Federals passed on.

At Beaver Dam Station, Stuart left his command a short while to see if his wife and children, who were near by at the home of Mr. Edmund Fontaine, had escaped annoyance from the Federals. Having found them safe and well, he pressed on toward Hanover Junction to place his forces between Sheridan and Richmond.

Hanover Junction was reached after dark and Stuart proposed an all-night march. Fitz Lee's men, however, were worn out with fighting and marching and, at the request of their commander, Stuart at last consented that the troopers should rest until one o'clock. He directed his trusted adjutant, Major McClellan, should remain awake to arouse the sleeping men, and to see them mounted and on the march at the time mentioned.

Major McClellan in his *Life of Stuart*, says: "When the troops had moved out, I returned to Stuart and awoke him and his staff. While they were preparing to move, I lay down to catch, if possible, a few moments' rest. The party rode off as I lay in a half-conscious condition, and I heard some one say, 'General, here's McClellan fast asleep. Must I wake him?' 'No' he replied, 'he has been watching while we were asleep. Leave a courier with him and tell him to come on when his nap is out.'"

After taking a short rest Major McClellan rejoined General Stuart just as he passed the road leading to Ashland. A squadron of Confederate cavalry had come upon a force of Federal cavalry in that town, and had dispersed it with great loss to the latter.

Stuart reached Yellow Tavern, about eight miles from Richmond, about ten o'clock on the morning of May 11. He had beaten Sheridan in the race to Richmond and placed himself between that city and Sheridan's forces. He at once posted his small force to meet the Federal advance. Wickham was placed on the right of the Telegraph Road and Lomax on the left. Two guns were placed in the road and one farther to the left. The whole force was dismounted, except a portion of the cavalry which was held in reserve.

General Stuart then sent Major McClellan into Richmond to find out the condition of affairs in the city. General Bragg, in charge of the defense, replied he had enough men to hold the trenches and he was hourly expecting reinforcements from Petersburg — that he wished General Stuart to remain on the Federal flank and to retard its progress as much as possible.

General Stuart's last official dispatch written on the morning of May 11, the day he was wounded, showed his wonderful determination and unfailing cheerfulness in the face of danger and difficulty, and was also a tribute to the men who fought under him.

He wrote: "May 11th, 1864, 6:30 A.M. Fighting against immense odds of Sheridan — my men and horses are tired, hungry, and jaded, *but all right.*"

About four o'clock that same day, Sheridan attacked the whole line, throwing a brigade of cavalry upon the left. Stuart galloped to this point, and found the Federals had captured his two guns and had driven back almost the entire left. He at once ordered a reserve squadron to charge the advancing Federals. Just as the latter were being driven back in a hand-to-hand combat, General Stuart rode up to where Captain Dorsey and about eighty dismounted men who had collected on the Telegraph Road, were firing at the retreating Federals. As the struggling mass fell back, one of the Federals who had been unhorsed in the fight, turned and fired his pistol directly at General Stuart. The fatal shot entered his body just above the sword-belt.

Captain Dorsey saw the general was wounded and hurried to his assistance. He tried to lead the general's horse to a safer place, but it became very unruly. General Stuart insisted on being lifted off and allowed to rest against a tree. Then he ordered the captain to go back to his men, but Captain Dorsey refused to do so until his general had been taken to the rear. There were now only a few of Stuart's men between him and the Federals and for a few moments there was great danger of his being captured.

But soon another horse was brought, and the general was taken to a safer place by Captain Dorsey and put in charge of Private Wheatley. Wheatley speedily procured an ambulance, and took the general to the rear. Here Dr, Fontaine and two of the general's aides, Venable and Hullihen, took charge of their wounded chief and started at once to Richmond.

As the ambulance passed through the disordered Confederate ranks the general called to his men, "Go back! go back and do your duty as I have done, and our country will be safe. Go back! go back! I had rather die than be whipped."

These were his last words upon the battlefield, and they carried to his men a message, full of the spirit of their beloved chief. They did 'go back,' and fought so well that Sheridan was finally driven from Richmond.

The ambulance had to take a rough and roundabout way, in order to avoid the Federals, and it did not reach Richmond until after dark. The general was taken to the home of his brother-in- law Dr. Charles Brewer. He had suffered greatly on the trip, but had borne the pain with fortitude and cheerfulness.

The next morning. Major McClellan, who according to Stuart's orders had remained on the battlefield, rode into the city to deliver to General Bragg a message from General Fitz Lee now in command of the cavalry. As soon as he had delivered his message, he went at once to the bedside of his wounded general. Inflammation had set in, and the doctors said there was no hope of Stuart's recovery. I shall let McClellan tell you in his own words about the general's last hours.

He says: "After delivering General Fitz Lee's message to General Bragg, I repaired to the bedside of my dying chief. He was calm and composed, in the full possession of his mind. Our conversation was, however, interrupted by paroxysms of suffering. He directed me to make the proper disposal of his official papers, and to send his personal effects to his wife.

"He then said: 'I wish you to take one of my horses and Venable the other. Which is the heavier rider?'

"I replied that I thought Venable was.

"Then he said, 'let Venable have the gray-horse and you take the bay.'

"Soon he spoke again: 'You will find in my hat a small Confederate flag, which a lady of Columbia, South Carolina, sent me, with the request that I would wear it upon my horse in a battle and then return it to her. Send it to her.'"

Later, Major McClellan found the flag inside the lining of the general's hat. Among his papers was the letter conveying the lady's request.

"Again he said: 'My spurs which I have always worn in battle, I promised to give to Mrs. Lilly Lee, of Shepherdstown, Virginia. My sword I leave to my son.'

"While I sat by his bed, the sound of cannon outside the city was heard. He turned to me eagerly and inquired what it meant. I explained that Gracey's brigade and other troops had moved out against the rear of the enemy on the Brooke turnpike and that Fitz Lee would endeavor to oppose their advance at Meadow Bridge.

"He turned his eyes upward, and exclaimed earnestly, 'God grant that they may be successful.' Then turning his head aside, he said with a sigh: 'But I must be prepared for another world.'

"The thought of duty was ever uppermost in his mind, and after listening to the distant cannonading for a few moments, he said, 'Major, Fitz Lee may need you.' I understood his meaning and pressed his hand in a last farewell. As I left his chamber. President Davis entered.

'Taking the general's hand he asked: 'General, how do you feel?'

"He replied: 'Easy, but willing to die if God and my country think I have fulfilled my destiny, and done my duty.'"

"The Rev. Dr. Peterkin visited him, and prayed with him. He requested Dr. Peterkin to sing *Rock of Ages*, and joined in the singing of the hymn.

The house where Stuart died. It has since been torn down.

"During the afternoon, he asked Dr. Brewer whether it were not possible for him to survive the night. The doctor frankly told him death was close at hand.

"He then said: 'I am resigned if it be God's will; but I would like to see my wife. But God's will be done.'

"Again he said to Dr. Brewer: 'I am going fast now; I am resigned. God's will be done.'"

Major Von Borcke, General Stuart's former aide who had not yet recovered from his severe wound, was also in Richmond. After McClellan went away, Von Borcke remained at his chieftain's side. He tells us he sat on the bed, holding the general's hand and handing him crushed ice which he ate in great abundance and which was applied to cool his burning wound. Everyone was hoping Mrs. Stuart would arrive in time to be with him before he passed from earth.

Finally the general drew Von Borcke to him, and after bidding him farewell said, "Look after my family after I am gone and be the same true friend to my wife and children that you have been to me." These were his last connected words.

At eight o'clock the end came, and it was three hours later before Mrs. Stuart arrived. The destruction of bridges and a fearful storm had caused delay in the trip from Beaver Dam. Owing to the telegraph lines being broken, the tidings that General Stuart was wounded did not reach his wife until noon on May 12.

At the time of his death, May 12, Stuart was just thirty-one years old. Yet through his high ideals, his devotion to duty, and his military genius, he had risen to a position of great trust and honor in the service of his country for which he laid down his life. Such a death, crowning such a life, is glorious and inspiring. One feels that Horatius, the noble Roman, in-deed spoke truly when he said:

> "And how can man die better,
> Than by facing fearful odds,
> For the ashes of his fathers
> And the temples of his gods?"

General J. E. B. Stuart

CHAPTER XIII
SOME TRIBUTES TO STUART

While General Stuart's life was ebbing away, General Sheridan retired from the attack on Richmond. The delay at Ashland and the all-day fight at Yellow Tavern in which two brigades of Stuart's cavalry had detained the ten thousand men of Sheridan's command, had given the authorities at Richmond time to collect forces for the defense of the city.

General Fitz Lee who now commanded the cavalry, harassed the retreat of Sheridan for a while, but his men and horses were too worn-out to attempt to cut off so large a force. Sheridan, therefore, marched through the swamps of the Chickahominy River to the Pamunkey, and after an absence of more than two weeks, rejoined Grant's army which was still vainly attempting to get between Lee and Richmond.

General Fitz Lee in his *Life of General Robert E. Lee,* says: "Sheridan's raid would have been the usual record of nothing accomplished and a broken-down command except that at Yellow Tavern the Confederate cavalry chieftain was mortally wounded and died the next day in Richmond. This sad occurrence was of more value to the Federal cause than anything that could have happened, and his loss to Lee was irreparable. He was the army's eyes and ears — vigilant always, bold to a fault, of great vigor and ceaseless activity. He had a heart ever loyal to his superior, and duty, was to him the 'sublimest word in the language.'"

In a letter to his wife a few days after General Stuart's death. General Robert E. Lee said: "As I write, I expect to hear the sound of guns every moment. I grieve for the loss of the gallant officers and men, and miss their aid and sympathy. A more zealous, ardent, brave, and devoted soldier than Stuart the Confederacy cannot have."

General Lee's order to the army announcing the death of Stuart was as follows: "Among the gallant soldiers who have fallen in the war. General Stuart was second to none in valor, in zeal, and in unflinching devotion to his country. His achievements form a conspicuous part of the history of this army, with which his name and services will be forever associated. To military capacity of a high order, he added the brighter graces of a pure life guided and sustained by the Christian's faith and hope. The mysterious hand of an all-wise God has removed him from the scene of his usefulness and fame. His grateful countrymen will mourn his loss and cherish his memory. To his comrades in arms he has left the proud recollection of his deeds and the inspiring influence of his example."

General Wade Hampton's order to his cavalry corps was also an eloquent tribute to the great cavalry leader. It was as follows:

"In the midst of rejoicing over the success of our arms, the sad tidings come to us from Richmond of the death of our distinguished Chief of Cavalry. Death has at last accepted the offering of a life, which before the admiring eyes of the Army, has been so often, so freely and so nobly offered, on almost every battlefield of Virginia. In the death of Major General J. E. B. Stuart the Army of Northern Virginia has lost one of its most brilliant, enthusiastic and zealous military leaders, the Southern cause one of its earliest, most untiring and devoted supporters, and the Cavalry arm of the service a chieftain who first gave it prominence and value, and whose dazzling achievements have attracted the wonder and applause of distant nations. His spirit shone as bright and brave in the still chamber of death, as amid the storm of the battlefield, and he passed out of life the same buoyant hero he had lived. Blessed through a short but glorious career with many instances of almost miraculous good fortune, it was his great privilege to die with the consciousness of having performed his whole duty to his country. To his children he leaves the rich legacy of a name which has become identified with the brightest acts of our military history and, when the panorama of our battles shall be unfolded to posterity, in almost every picture will be seen the form of our gallant leader. His name will be associated with almost every scene of danger and of glory, in which the Cavalry of the Virginia Army has borne a part, and they will recount the exploits of Stuart with the pride which men feel in their own honorable records.

"The Major General commanding hopes that this division will show by their own noble conduct their high appreciation of the character of their lost commander, and when the danger thickens around them and the cause of their country calls for heroic efforts they will remember the example of Stuart. No leader ever set a more glorious example to his soldiers on the battlefield than he did, and it becomes the men he has so often led, while they mourn his fall, to emulate his courage, to imitate his heroic devotion to duty and to avenge his death."

While General Lee and his army continued to wrestle with the hosts of Grant, the city of Richmond was in deep gloom and mourning. Once more the tide of battle had come near her gates; and this time the beloved and gallant Stuart had fallen. He had been the pride of her heart, her brave and chivalrous defender. But Stuart was to sleep his last long sleep upon her bosom, in beautiful Hollywood around whose promontories sweep the waters of the James as they rush onward to the Chesapeake and where the tall pine trees whisper of the life eternal. The city aroused herself from her grief to do homage to the noble dead.

The City Council of Richmond passed resolutions of respect and sympathy for the family of General Stuart and asked the body of him who "yielded up his heroic spirit in the immediate defense of their city, and the successful effort to purchase their safety by the sacrifice of his own life," might "be permitted to rest under the eye and guardianship of the people of Richmond and that they might be allowed to commemorate by a suitable monument their gratitude and his services."

At five o'clock on the afternoon of May 13, the funeral of General Stuart took place from old St. James Church in Richmond. The coffin containing the remains of the brave soldier was carried up the aisle and, covered with wreaths and flowers, was placed before the altar.

The funeral service was conducted by Reverend Dr. Peterkin who had been with General Stuart during his last hours. The church was filled with officials of the Confederate government and citizens of Richmond. President Davis sat near the front, with a look of great sadness upon his careworn face. His cabinet officers were around him and on either side of the church were the senators and representatives of the Confederate Congress. But the cavalry officers and soldiers who loved and followed Stuart were all absent. They were on the firing line, either in the Wilderness or on the Chickahominy,— fighting in defense of Richmond which he had died to save.

No military escort could be spared from the front to accompany the funeral procession to Hollywood or to fire the usual parting salute to the dead commander. But as the body was lowered into the grave, the earth trembled with the roar of artillery from the battlefield where his old troops were obeying his last command and driving back the Federals. No better salute could have been given the gallant leader.

Stuart's grave in Hollywood Cemetery, Richmond, VA.

Leaving the body of their brave defender beneath the pines of Hollywood, the officials and citizens of Richmond returned to their homes to meet other sorrows. Before a year passed, the devoted city was overtaken by the fate which Stuart had so ably aided Lee in averting. Richmond fell into the hands of the Federals, General Lee surrendered, and the Southern Confederacy was no more.

When the city arose from her ashes and again put on the garb of peace, one of her first works was to erect memorials in honor of the men who had fought so nobly in her defense.

In 1888, a monument was erected by some of Stuart's comrades to mark the place at Yellow Tavern where he received his mortal wound. Governor Fitzhugh Lee was the orator of the occasion. He had been one of Stuart's most trusted brigadier generals, and had known him since they were cadets together at West Point.

In beautiful and touching language, he reviewed the chief events of Stuart's life, his brilliant campaigns, and his last hours.

The shaft at Yellow Tavern is twenty-two feet high and stands on a knoll about thirty feet from the spot where Stuart was wounded. Upon it are the following inscriptions:

Face: Upon this field, Major-Genl. J. E. B. Stuart, Commander Confederate Cavalry A. N. Va., received his mortal wound, May 11, 1864.

Right: He was fearless and faithful, pure and powerful, tender and true.

Left: This stone is erected by some of his comrades to commemorate his valor.

Rear: He saved Richmond, but he gave his life. Born Feb. 6, 1833, died May 12, 1864.

In 1891, the "Veteran Cavalry Association of the Army of Northern Virginia" was organized for the purpose of marking the grave of General Stuart with a suitable monument; but it was afterwards decided, with the aid of the city of Richmond, the association would erect an equestrian statue. The city donated the site on Monument Avenue, near the equestrian statue of General Lee, and also contributed a large sum of money, so that the association was enabled to erect the statue.

The sculptor, Mr. Fred Moynihan, designed and executed a statue, which is an excellent likeness of General Stuart and a striking example of the sculptor's skill. In 1907, the memorial was unveiled in the presence of an immense concourse of people, including large numbers of veterans from all parts of the South. Chief among the guests of honor were Miss Mary Custis Lee, Mrs. Stonewall Jackson, and Mrs. J. E. B. Stuart.

Fully ten thousand men marched in the column which took more than an hour to pass a given point. Veterans who were too feeble to endure the fatigue of the march went early to the monument, and joined the great multitude that crowded the sidewalks and even the housetops.

When the parade reached the monument, the crowd was so dense it was with difficulty the police made way for the orator and distinguished guests. The multitude was called to order by Major Andrew R. Venable, of Farmville, Virginia, a member of the staff of General Stuart, who introduced Rev. Walter Q. Hullihen, of Staunton, Virginia, another member of Stuart's staff, who made the dedicatory prayer. Major Venable then introduced the orator of the day, Judge Theodore S. Garnett of Norfolk, Virginia, another member of the staff of General Stuart.

It was indeed a remarkable incident that three of General Stuart's staff officers presided at the unveiling of his statue forty-three years after his death.

Judge Garnett in an eloquent speech reviewed the life and campaigns of Stuart, paying glowing tributes to the general, to the "ever-glorious and gallant" Stuart Horse Artillery, and to his comrades of Mosby's Battalion. He closed with these words: "To the city of Richmond, as its faithful guardian, we commit this monument, in whose care and keeping it will henceforth stand in token of a people's gratitude and in perpetual memory of his heroic name."

The veil was then drawn from the monument by the hand of little Virginia Stuart Waller, General Stuart's granddaughter. As the canvas fell from the heroic figure of General Stuart mounted on his powerful horse, the guns of the Howitzers boomed a salute and the cheering of the vast throng arose in billows of sound.

"Stuart was again riding with Lee!"

Stuart statue on Monument Avenue, Richmond, VA.

Monument at Yellow Tavern marking the place where Stuart was wounded.

SUGGESTIVE QUESTIONS

Chapter I

Give three incidents to prove that Stuart inherited his spirit of patriotism and devotion to duty.

Tell an interesting story connected with his grandmother, Bethenia Letcher Pannill.

What do you know of Stuart's life at Laurel Hill?

Tell what you can about his early education.

Give an account of his life at West Point.

What do you know of his religious feelings and convictions?

Tell about his choice of a profession and his equipment for it.

Chapter II

How did Stuart win distinction in his first military service?

What good qualities for a soldier and leader did he show in this adventure?

What two events of deep personal interest happened to Stuart in the fall of 1855?

Tell about the political trouble in Kansas at this time.

Who was "Ossawatomie" Brown?

Tell about Stuart's being wounded in a fight with Indians.

What qualities did he show in leading the party back to Fort Kearny?

What was the reason for his visit to Washington in 1859?

What interesting and important outcome did this visit have?

What feelings were aroused in the country by the John Brown Raid and the hanging of Brown?

Chapter III

What was Stuart's first cavalry commission under the Confederate government?

What kind of troops did he have, and what was his work?

Tell about his wonderful capture at Falling Waters.

What did General Joseph E. Johnston say about Stuart?

Tell about Stuart's part in the First Battle of Manassas.

Tell about the visits paid Stuart by his family at his outpost near Washington.

What did General Longstreet write President Davis about Stuart?

Chapter IV

See if you can paint a word-picture of Stuart when he was made a brigadier general.

Why did the soldiers still keep their confidence in Stuart after his defeat at the battle of Dranesville?

What was the Peninsular Campaign? What was Stuart's part in it, up to the time that General Lee was made commander of the Army of Northern Virginia?

Describe the Chickahominy Raid. Why is this raid one of the most wonderful cavalry achievements in history?

Tell two interesting incidents connected with the capture of the Federal supply depot at the White House.

Tell about the close of the Peninsular Campaign.

Chapter V

What was Stuart's reward for his services in the Peninsular Campaign?

Tell about the reorganization of the cavalry.

Give an account of life at Dundee. What brought it to a close?

Tell about the capture of Stuart's hat.

Give an account of the adventure in which he "made the Yankees pay for that hat."

What was Stuart's part in the Second Battle of Manassas?

Chapter VI

Tell about the capture of Fairfax Courthouse.

Tell a story to show how the people of this section felt toward General Stuart and the cause for which he fought.

Describe the crossing of the cavalry into Maryland.

Do you think the Maryland people were glad to welcome the Confederates into their State? Why?

Tell about the ball at Urbana.

How did the Confederates treat the Unionists in Frederick?

Describe Stuart's retreat from Frederick to South Mountain.

What were the principal mountain passes and why was it necessary for the cavalry to hold them until the capture of Harper's Ferry?

What did General Jackson say about General Stuart at the battle of Sharpsburg?

How did the cavalry help General Lee to get his army back safely into Virginia?

Tell about "the girl of Williamsport."

Tell about Stuart and Von Borcke's narrow escape from being captured on a reconnoitering expedition.

Tell about Bob Sweeny and camp life at The Bower.

Chapter VII

Would you have been proud of being one of the soldiers chosen by Stuart to accompany him on the Chambersburg Raid? Why?

Give a brief account of the raid.

To whom did Stuart assign all the glory and honor?

What was the effect of the raid on the North? On the South?

Why was Stuart sometimes called "Knight of the Golden Spurs?"

Chapter VIII

Tell about McClellan's campaign in the autumn of 1862 and the retreat of the cavalry toward Culpeper.

What exciting adventure did Stuart have at Ashby's Gap?

What qualities as a man and a soldier did Stuart show during the illness and after the death of his "little Flora"?

When and how did Stuart lose a part of his mustache?

What was the condition of Stuart's cavalry at the time Burnside took McClellan's place as commander of the Federal army?

Tell about the snowball fight in the Confederate camp at Fredericksburg.

What part did Stuart and his cavalry take in the battle of Fredericksburg?

How did Pelham, the young chief of the Stuart Horse Artillery, distinguish himself in this battle?

Tell about the Dumfries Raid and the joke that Stuart played on the Federal quartermaster at Washington.

Tell about the friendship between Stuart and Jackson.

What changes took place in the Federal army in the early spring of 1863?

Chapter IX

Tell about the death of young Pelham and Stuart's love for him.

Give an account of Stuart's encounters with the Federal cavalry just before the battle of Chancellorsville.

How did Stuart and his cavalry assist Jackson in surprising the Federal left flank?

When Jackson was wounded, what did he say about Stuart?

How did Stuart fulfill Jackson's trust?

Tell about Stoneman's raid and its result.

Chapter X

Describe the Culpeper cavalry review.

Draw a diagram showing how the Federals gave Stuart a double surprise in the battle of Fleetwood Hill, or Brandy Station, attacking him from both the front and the rear.

Describe the final combat for the possession of the hill.

Chapter XI

Why did Lee's plan prevent Stuart's following up Pleasanton's retreat?

Why did not Stuart follow the route of the remainder of the army when he started into Pennsylvania to join Early at York?

Describe his march from Seneca Ford to Carlisle.

In the light of what he knew, would it have been wise for Stuart to abandon his captured wagons? Give a reason for your opinion.

How long did his saving the wagons delay his march?

Do you think he would have kept the wagons if he had known what was happening at Gettysburg?

What part did Stuart and his cavalry take in the third day's battle?

Tell about the work of Stuart and his cavalry in covering the retreat of General Lee's army.

Tell the incident about Stuart and the hard-boiled eggs.

Explain his conduct on this occasion.

Chapter XII

Tell about General Lee's position and Stuart's encounter with Buford and Kilpatrick at Jack's Shop.

What was the "Bristoe Campaign?"

Tell how Stuart drove the Federals a second time from Fleetwood Hill.

What narrow escape did Stuart and his cavalry have near Catlett's Station?

Tell about Virginia Pelham Stuart.

What northern general took command of all the Federal armies in the spring of 1864?

Tell about the Battle of the Wilderness. What interesting anecdote is told about Stuart when he was on his way to this battle?

Tell about the battle of Spotsylvania Courthouse.

How did General Stuart try to save Major McClellan from danger in this battle?

Describe the cavalry raid that General Grant planned in order to take Richmond.

How did Stuart beat Sheridan in the race to Yellow Tavern?

Tell about Stuart's being wounded and borne from the field.

What was his last command to his men?

What impressed you most when you read the account of Stuart's death?

Why is such a death as this glorious and inspiring?

Repeat the lines from "Horatius" that apply to the death of Stuart.

Chapter XIII

What tribute did Fitz Lee pay his dead commander?

What private and public tributes were paid by General Robert E. Lee?

How did the city of Richmond show her grief at the time of Stuart's death?

What later tributes has she given to her hero and defender?

THE ORGANIZATION OF AN ARMY

The Federal and Confederate armies in the War of Secession were organized in practically the same way. There were a few points of difference, and in active service the numbers and arrangement of military forces varied and were changed.

INFANTRY

Squad: any small number of men, usually 7, under command of a corporal.

Platoon: a subdivision, usually half, of a company under a lieutenant.

Company: from 83 to 125 men under a captain.

Battalion: 2 or more, usually four, companies under a major.

Regiment: 10 companies—or 3 battalions of 4 companies each — under a colonel or a lieutenant-colonel.

Brigade: 3 to 5 regiments under a brigadier-general.

Division: 2 to 5 brigades under a major-general.

Army corps: 2 or more divisions under a major-general or a lieutenant-general — organized as a complete army and sufficient in itself for all the operations of war.

CAVALRY

Squad: any small number of men, usual 7, under a corporal.

Platoon: a sub-division, usually half, of a company under a lieutenant.

Troop: 2 to 6 platoons, 76 to 100 men, under a captain.

Squadron: 2 to 4 troops under a senior captain or a major.

Regiment: 10 troops — or 4 to 6 squadrons —u nder a colonel.

Brigade: 3 or 4 regiments under a brigadier-general.

Division: 2 to 4 brigades under a major-general.

ARTILLERY

Battery: usually 144 men with 4 guns and 2 howitzers, under a captain.

Battalion: 3 to 4 batteries under a major.

Regiment: 2 to 8 battalions under a colonel.

When infantry regiments are combined into brigades, brigades into divisions, and divisions into army corps — cavalry, artillery, and certain other auxiliary troops, such as engineers, signal corps, etc., are joined with them in such proportions as are necessary. Every unit, from the company up, has its own supply and ammunition wagons, field hospitals, etc.

WORD LIST

Ab o li′tion party: a political party, founded by Garrison about 1833, the object of which was to free all slaves in the United States.

ad vănçe′: forward movement of a military force.

advance guard: troops which march in front, in order to secure a military force against surprise.

āid′-dē-cămp: an officer who assists a general by sending orders, collecting information, etc.

āide: a military or naval officer who assists a superior officer.

A pä′che: a warlike Indian tribe originally located in New Mexico and Arizona.

är′se nal: a place for the storage or manufacture of arms and military equipment.

ar tĭl′ler y: cannon, large or small; that branch of the service which handles the cannon.

as sault′: attack of a military force on the works or position of an enemy, in the effort to carry it by a single charge.

bāse: a place from which the operations of an army proceed, forward movements are made, supplies are furnished, etc.

bat tăl′ion: See page 119.

bat′ter y: See page 119.

bĭv′ouac (-wăk): a temporary encampment of soldiers, usually without tents.

bri gāde′: See page 119.

brŭnt: the shock of an attack or onset.

buoy′ant: cheerful, light-hearted.

cāis′ son: a strong four-wheeled wagon, consisting of two parts, the body and the limber, that carries ammunition chests or boxes.

căn′is ter: cannon shot consisting of a metal cylinder which bursts when fired, discharging the bullets with which it is filled.

cär′bine: a short, light rifle used chiefly by cavalry.

căs'ca bel: a knob or projection in the rear of the breech of a muzzle-loading cannon.

căv'al ry: that part of the army consisting of mounted soldiers.

Çheȳ ĕnne': an Indian tribe formerly inhabiting South Dakota, Wyoming, and Nevada.

com man dänt': the commanding officer of a place or of a body of men.

cóm'pa ny: See page 119.

corps (cōr): See page 119.

coun'ter movement: a movement by which a body of troops marches back over ground it has recently occupied or marched over.

cŭl'mi nat ed: reached a final result.

di vĭ'sion: See page 119.

en cămped: formed a camp.

en trĕnch': fortify with defensive works as with a trench or ditch and a wall.

en trĕnch'ments: fortifications consisting of a parapet of earth and the ditch or trench from which the earth was taken.

flănk: the side of an army, either in column or in line.

grāpe'shot: a cluster of iron balls arranged in an iron framework to be discharged from a cannon. Formerly grapeshot was enclosed in a canvas bag so quilted as to look like a bunch of grapes.

guī'dons: small flags carried by cavalry and field artillery.

hăv'er sack: a bag or case in which a soldier carries provisions on a march.

Ho rā'tius: a hero of ancient Rome who with two others defended the bridge across the Tiber against an advancing army. Read Lord Macaulay's poem *Horatius*.

how'itz er: a cannon for throwing shells.

ĭm' mi nent: threatening; dangerous and close at hand.

in dŏm'i ta ble: unyielding; unconquerable.

ĭn'fan try: foot soldiers armed with rifles and bayonets; one of the three chief divisions of an army, the other two being cavalry and artillery.

in vĕst'ing: surrounding with troops; laying siege to.

ir rĕp'a ra ble: not capable of being repaired or remedied.

lăr'i at: a long, small rope used for catching or for picketing cattle or horses.

lĭm'ber: the fore part of a gun carriage, consisting of a chest mounted on two wheels and having a pole for the horses. See caisson.

ma neū'vers: movements or changes of position of troops or war-vessels for tactical purposes or for display.

ma rīnes': naval troops; soldiers serving on war-vessels.

mär'tial law: the military administration which when proclaimed takes the place of civil law in time of war or disorder.

mĭl'i ta ry law: the laws by which an army and its affairs are governed. Military law differs from martial law in that the former is a permanent code for the government of the army and the latter is the application of the laws of war to all the people in a certain district.

mīne: an explosive charge, sunken in the earth or under water, for the purpose of destroying an enemy passing over it — formerly exploded by contact or by a fuse, but now usually exploded by electricity.

ôrd'nance: military supplies.

ŏr'i flămme: a standard or ensign in battle, especially the ancient royal banner of France.

out'post: a post or station outside the limits of a camp, for observation or to guard against surprise.

pa rōled': set at liberty on parole, or word of honor not to bear arms against the captors.

pĕr'emp to ry: authoritative; not admitting of debate or question.

pĭck'ets: soldiers stationed on the outskirts of a camp to warn against the enemy's approach.

pīkes: soldiers' weapons, consisting of wooden staves with steel points. In recent warfare, pikes have been superceded by bayonets.

pla tōōn': See page 119.

pon tōōn': a vessel, such as a flat-bottomed boat or a canvas covered frame, used in the construction of a floating bridge.

pre dĭc'a ment: a difficult or trying condition or situation.

prō'vost (vō) guard: a body of soldiers detailed for police duties.

qua r'ter master: a staff officer of a regiment or other body of troops, whose duty it is to provide quarters, arrange transportation, and provide and issue food, clothing, and other supplies.

rănk: grade of official standing in the army or navy.

rēar guard: troops which march in the rear of a body of forces in order to protect it.

re cŏn'na is sănçe: an examination of territory or of an enemy's position for the purpose of gaining information — sometimes involving an attack for the purpose of discovering the enemy's position and strength.

rĕg'i ment: See page 119.

re trēat': the withdrawal, especially in an orderly manner, of troops from an exposed or dangerous position.

rī'fled: having the bore rifled, or grooved spirally, in order to give a rotary motion to the bullet.

shĕll: a hollow projectile for cannon, which contains an explosive charge.

sīde arms: weapons worn at the side or in the belt, as sword, pistol, bayonet, etc., especially sword.

Sĭd'ney, Sir Philip: a famous English soldier and author of the sixteenth century, the model of unselfish courage. He was mortally wounded in battle of Zulphen in 1586.

sī mul tā'ne ous: happening at the same time.

spȳ: a soldier not in uniform who penetrates the enemy's camp or zone of operations, for the purpose of gaining information.

tăl'ma: a style of long cape or cloak worn by men and women during the first half of the nineteenth century.

un lĭm'ber ed: removed from the limber. See limber and caisson.

Zou äves': infantry wearing a brilliant oriental uniform, consisting of leggings, baggy trousers, short jacket, and tasseled cap or turban.

Other publications from

The Scuppernong Press

www.scuppernongpress.com

Lincoln As The South Should Know Him
....O. W. Blacknall

Truth of the War Conspiracy of 1861
....H. W. Johnstone

A Story Behind Every Stone
.... Charles E. Purser

As You May Never See Us Again
.... Joel Craig and Sharlene Baker

Additional Information and Amendments to the North Carolina Troops 1861 – 1865 Volume I & II
.... Charles E. Purser

Memoir of Nathaniel Macon of North Carolina......... Weldon N. Edwards

Sherman's Rascals..Frank B. Powell, III

A Southern View of the Invasion of the Southern States and War of 1861-65 .... Captain Samuel A. Ashe

A Confederate Catechism ....Lyon Gardiner Tyler

General Robert E. Lee .... Captain Samuel A. Ashe

General Lee and Santa Claus..Louise Clack

The Life of Nathaniel Macon ....William E. Dodd

The Land We Love — The South and It's Heritage............ Dr. Boyd Cathey

Pickett or Pettigrew? An Historical Essay......................Captain W. R. Bond

A View of the Constitution of the United States of America
....William Rawle

The Confederate Myth-Buster... Walter D. Kennedy

Confederate States Military Prison at Salisbury, NC... Dr. A. W. Mangum

Red State — Red County..James R. Kennedy

Some Things For Which The South Did Not Fight
.... Dr. Henry Tucker Graham

The Retribution Conspiracy... Samuel W. Mitcham

Little Sermons in Socialism by Abraham Lincoln ....Burke McCarty

Roster of North Carolinians in Confederate Naval Service
.... LTC. (Retired) Sion H. Harrington, III

Words of Love ....Rev. Dr. W. Herman White

The Constitution of the Confederate States of America......................... CSA

The Adventure — Stolen Days .... Mark Vogl

Sketch of the Twelfth Alabama Infantry........................ Robert Emory Park

Experience of a Confederate Chaplain .... Rev. A. D. Betts

Loring's Division.. Ross Massey

The Life of General Robert E. Lee For Children........... Mary L. Williamson

California Knights of the Golden Circle .... Dr. Ted Boyas

The Life of General Thomas J. Jackson for Children... Mary L. Williamson

If Lee Had Not Won Gettysburg..Winston Churchill

Plymouth's Civil War..John Bernhard Theursam

Treasured Stories of the War Between The States.................Dr. Tony Zeiss

Backcountry Fury.. Dr. Tony Zeiss

More Treasured Stories of the War Between the States......... Dr. Tony Zeiss

California in the War for Southern Independence
....Dr. Laurence F. Talbott

Final Roll Call...Wade Sokolosky

Tribute to the Confederate Secret Service.................................. Dr. Ted Boyas

To Live and Die in Dixie............................... Sons of Confederate Veterans

Paradox of Freedom ....Larry Allen McCluney, Jr.

More information available at
www.scuppernongpress.com

The Scuppernong Press
PO Box 1724
Wake Forest, NC 27588

www.ingramcontent.com/pod-product-compliance
Lightning Source LLC
Chambersburg PA
CBHW070240090526
44586CB00035B/1249